Nancy Hall

Spell*well*

Book *Cc*

Educators Publishing Service, Inc.
Cambridge and Toronto

Cover design by Hugh Price

Illustrations by Alan Price and Hugh Price

Educators Publishing Service, Inc.
31 Smith Place, Cambridge, MA 02138-1089

Copyright © 2001, 1997 by Educators Publishing Service, Inc. All rights reserved. No part of this book may be reproduced or utilized in any form or by any electronic means, including photocopying, without permission in writing from the publisher.

Printed in the U.S.A.

ISBN 0-8388-2196-0

May 2001 Printing

CONTENTS

Copy the words your teacher gives you under Classroom Words. Fold this page back along the dotted line so that only the Pretest column shows. Write the words your teacher dictates.

Spell*well* Words	**Corrections**	**Pretest**
1. angry	____________	1. ____________
2. clumsy	____________	2. ____________
3. delivery	____________	3. ____________
4. diary	____________	4. ____________
5. duty	____________	5. ____________
6. enemy	____________	6. ____________
7. energy	____________	7. ____________
8. galaxy	____________	8. ____________
9. library	____________	9. ____________
10. memory	____________	10. ____________
11. mystery	____________	11. ____________
12. slippery	____________	12. ____________
13. tasty	____________	13. ____________
Outlaw Word		
14. survey	____________	14. ____________
Classroom Words		
15. ____________	____________	15. ____________
16. ____________	____________	16. ____________
17. ____________	____________	17. ____________
18. ____________	____________	18. ____________

Compare your words with the spelling list. Write the words you did not know in the Corrections column. If all, or all but one, of the words are correct, use the following for your spelling words: **ebony, energetic, memorized, petrify, solitary,** and **territory.** Write them in the Corrections column along with the Classroom Words; then do the Alternative Homework this week.

Find and circle the spelling words hidden on the computer screen. The words may be horizontal or vertical, but they do *not* overlap. Write the words on the lines below.

x d c l u m s y i h r e p r y g o b v n u k i l u

m b r m o e l t s m l o t r e w s c e s b m z a d

t o a z a d v e m e m o r y a l i l u y t r w k e

a s n c x o l l i n h a y s a d i a r y h t e p l

s s g q u e i a w e e s n c i o l e t r e s r c i

t e r t n s u r v e y p c o d f p e n e m y r l v

y s y o s s e n e r g y h e e g f o r e s p y k e

a b i c k r q e b m j y e s l i p p e r y g i t r

o u g a l a x y n k h s a s c o e s y o l l p g y

c d k t o l i b r a r y h e s t m i n b r o p l i

d u t y o l j i g h m e l w o m y s t e r y n a c

1. ________________
2. ________________
3. ________________
4. ________________
5. ________________
6. ________________
7. ________________
8. ________________
9. ________________
10. ________________
11. ________________
12. ________________
13. ________________
14. ________________

<u>ALTERNATIVE HOMEWORK</u> In your reading book find 8 words ending in *y* that you want to learn. Write them in the Corrections column on page 1. Then write all of your spelling words and their definitions in your personal dictionary.

Read the definitions below. Find the spelling words that fit the meanings and write the syllables in the spaces.

1. Delicious ___ ___ ___ + ___ ___
2. A task or necessary job ___ ___ + ___ ___
3. Furious; mad ___ ___ + ___ ___ ___
4. A baffling story ___ ___ ___ + ___ ___ ___ + ___
5. Likely to cause sliding ___ ___ ___ ___ + ___ ___ ___ + ___
6. To study in detail ___ ___ ___ + ___ ___ ___
7. Ability to remember ___ ___ ___ + ___ ___ + ___
8. Not a friend; a foe ___ ___ + ___ + ___ ___
9. Awkward ___ ___ ___ ___ + ___ ___
10. Strength to work or do things ___ ___ + ___ ___ + ___ ___
11. A written record of daily activities ___ ___ + ___ + ___ ___
12. A very large group of stars ___ ___ ___ + ___ ___ + ___
13. A place that lends books ___ ___ + ___ ___ ___ + ___ ___
14. Taking something to another place ___ ___ + ___ ___ ___ + ___ ___ + ___

Write sentences using your Classroom Words.

____

____

____

____

<u>ALTERNATIVE HOMEWORK</u> Write your spelling words in syllables. Then write questions using eight of the words. Trade papers with a classmate and answer each other's questions.

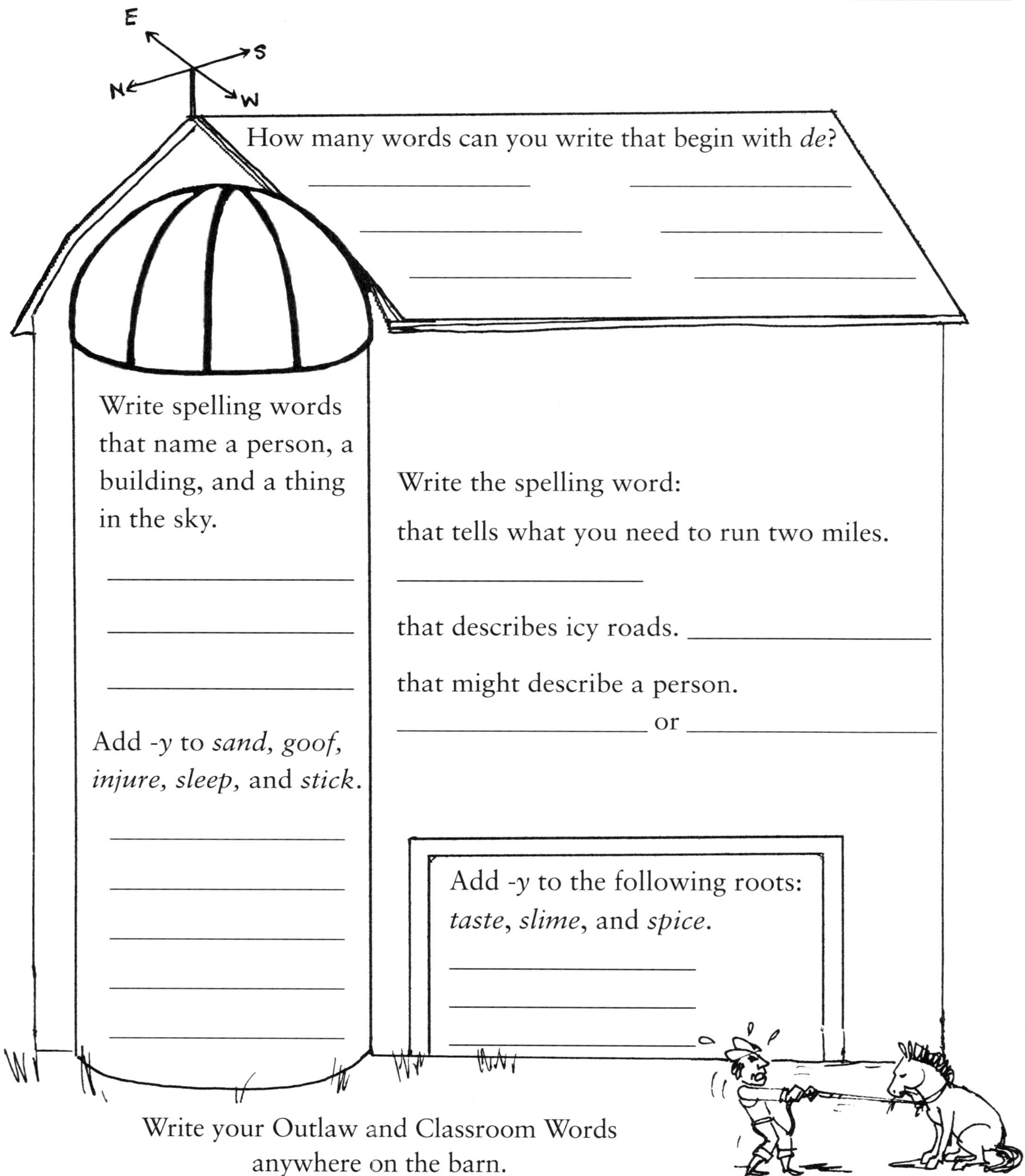

Write your Outlaw and Classroom Words anywhere on the barn.

ALTERNATIVE HOMEWORK Add any ending or prefix to your spelling words, and write the new words on the spaces above. If you cannot add anything, just write the spelling word.

Be a newspaper reporter. Write a paragraph about your school cafeteria. Describe what it looks like; then tell what is both good and bad about it. Use at least five spelling words in your article.

ARCHERY PRACTICE

Write each spelling word your teacher dictates in the space with the correct beginning letter and the right number of blanks.

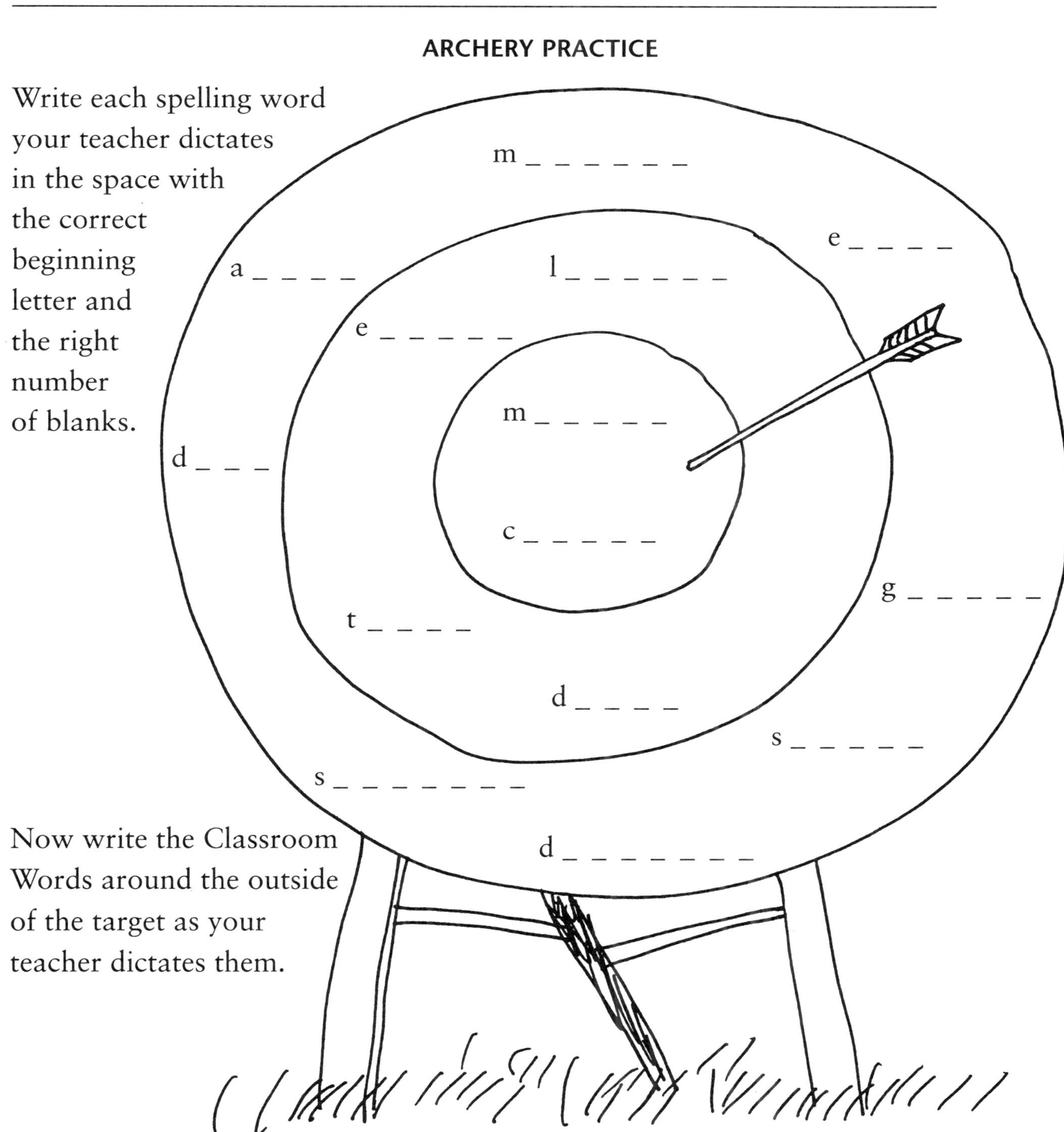

Now write the Classroom Words around the outside of the target as your teacher dictates them.

Be sure to study your spelling words for the test tomorrow!

ALTERNATIVE HOMEWORK Complete both activities above.

Copy the words your teacher gives you under Classroom Words. Fold this page back along the dotted line so that only the Pretest column shows. Write the words your teacher dictates.

Pretest	Corrections	Spell*well* Words
1. ________	________	1. **batteries**
2. ________	________	2. **fried**
3. ________	________	3. **happiness**
4. ________	________	4. **hobbies**
5. ________	________	5. **married**
6. ________	________	6. **puppies**
7. ________	________	7. **replying**
8. ________	________	8. **satisfied**
9. ________	________	9. **sloppiness**
10. ________	________	10. **studying**
11. ________	________	11. **trickiest**
12. ________	________	12. **trying**
13. ________	________	13. **windiest**
		Outlaw Words
14. ________	________	14. **business**
15. ________	________	15. **busy**
		Classroom Words
16. ________	________	16. ________
17. ________	________	17. ________
18. ________	________	18. ________

Compare your words with the spelling list. Write the words you did not know in the Corrections column. If all, or all but one, of the words are correct, use the following for your spelling words: **apologies, carriage, dutiful, mightiest, scurried, studious** and **x-rayed.** Write them in the Corrections column along with the Classroom Words; then do the Alternative Homework this week.

Circle the endings in the words below. Write the roots or base words on the spacecraft.

happiness business sloppiness

fried married satisfied

trickiest

puppies hobbies batteries

studying replying trying

windiest

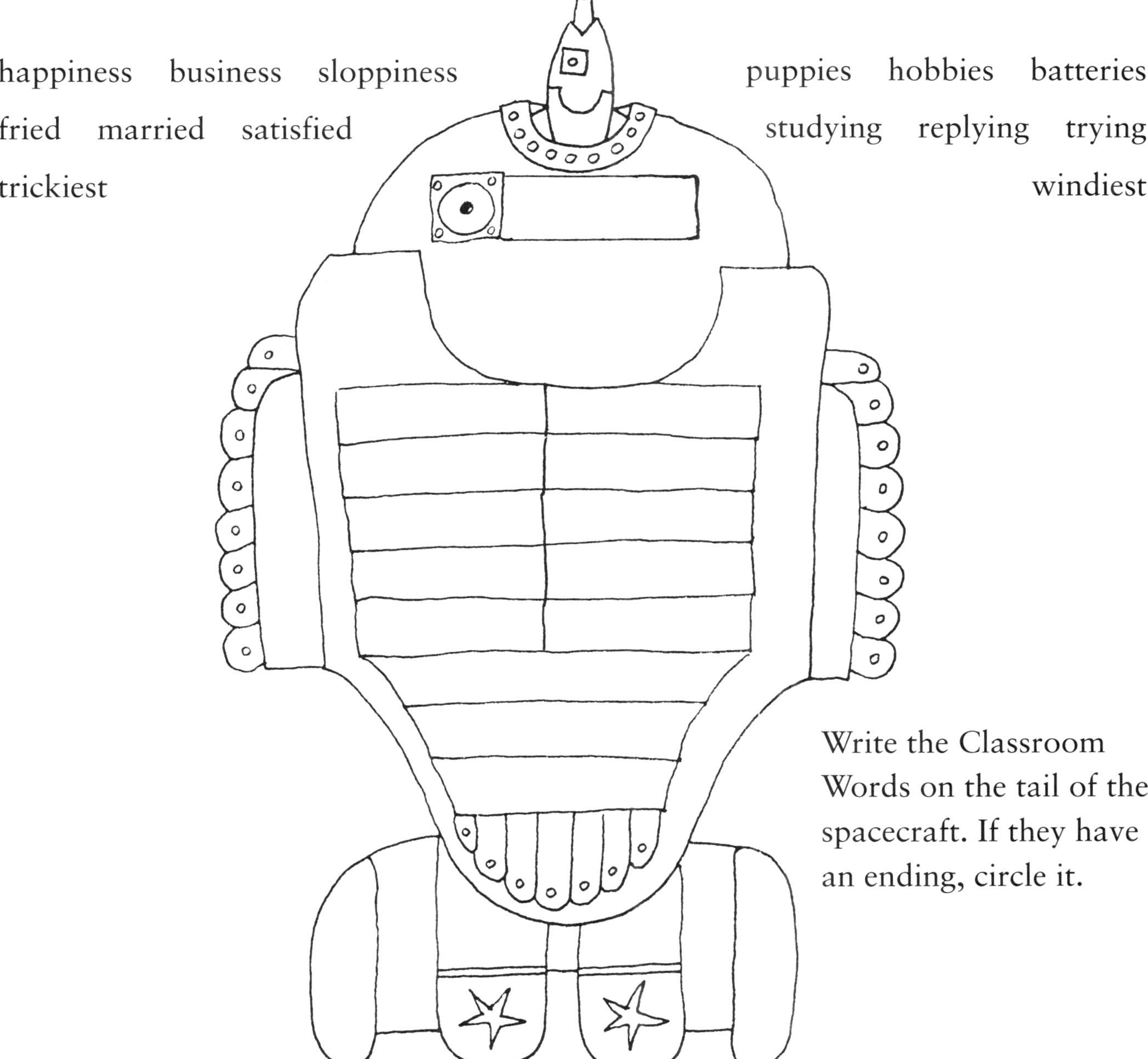

Write the Classroom Words on the tail of the spacecraft. If they have an ending, circle it.

> Look at the words above and then finish writing the rule below.
>
> **RULE:** When adding an ending to a word that ends in *y*, change the *y* to ____,
> except when the ending is ____.

ALTERNATIVE HOMEWORK In your reading book find 8 words that you want to learn. Write these words in the Corrections column on page 6. Then write all of your spelling words and their definitions in your personal dictionary.

Sometimes words can change meanings the way chameleons change color. Write the correct spelling word for each blank; then circle the meaning the word has in that sentence.

1. Gave enough to meet the need *or* convinced by.

   Rohan's parents were ____________________ with his excuse for being late.

2. The work a person does *or* one's matters or affairs.

   Don't meddle in other people's ____________________ .

3. Groups of similar things to be used together *or* devices that produce electricity.

   Flashlights must have ____________________ to work.

4. Fussy and cluttered-looking *or* occupied with work.

   The room looked ____________________ with so many pictures on every wall.

5. Examining in a court of law *or* making an effort; attempting.

   Chris is ____________________ to move the box alone, but it is too heavy.

6. Breeziest; having high winds *or* most boastful and talkative.

   We chose the ____________________ day to fly our kites.

7. Looking at closely *or* learning by reading and thinking.

   Detective Johnson was ____________________ the broken lock on the door.

8. Messiness or untidiness *or* carelessness.

   Lilly's addition error was caused by ____________________ .

9. Hardest in an unexpected way *or* most sly or cunning.

   The last problem on the test was the ____________________ .

Write your Classroom Words next to the chameleon.

<u>ALTERNATIVE HOMEWORK</u> Write a story about your favorite holiday. Be sure to include specific details that tell when it is, where you celebrate it, what kind of things you do, and why it is your choice. Try to use some spelling words in your story.

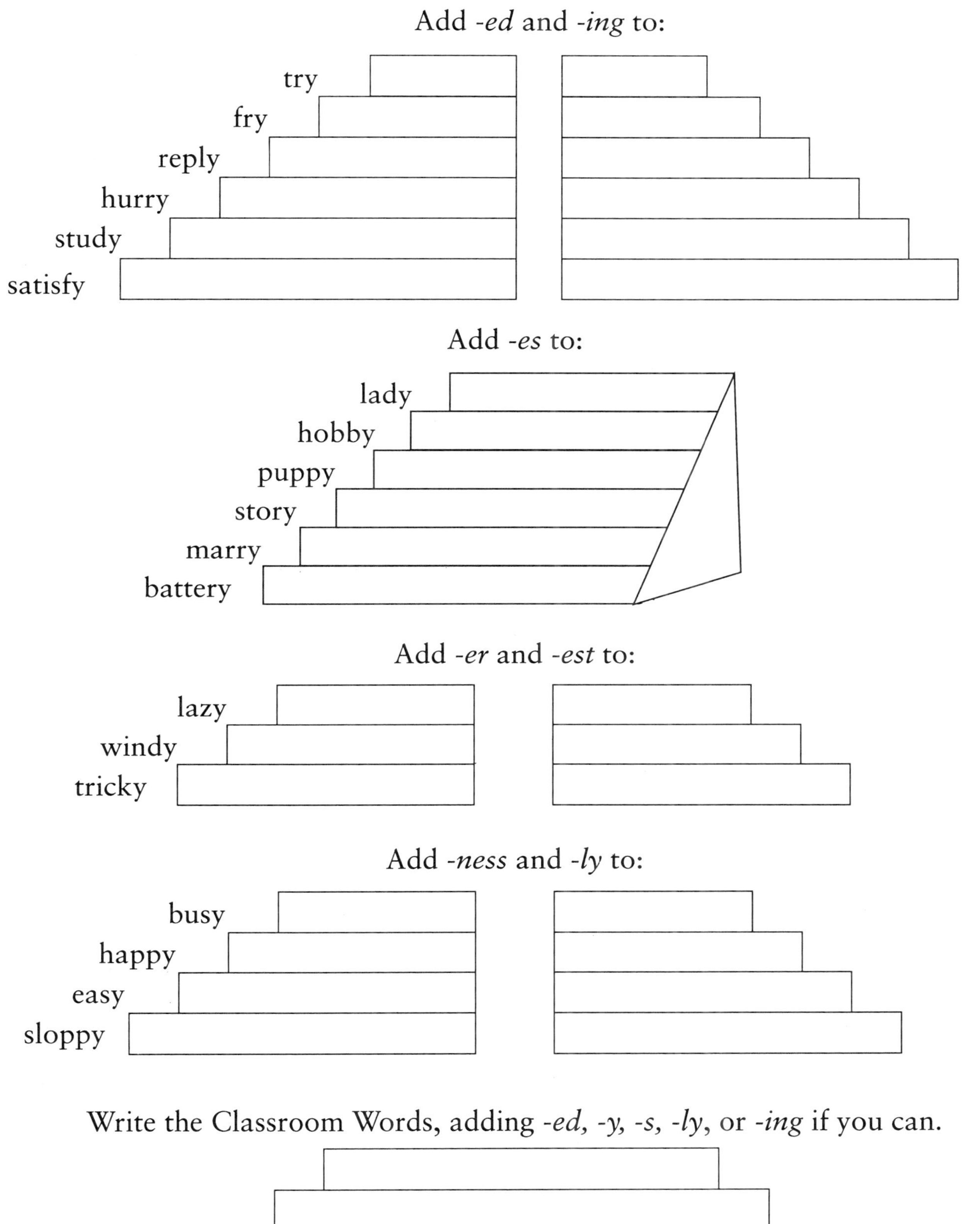

Write the Classroom Words, adding -*ed*, -*y*, -*s*, -*ly*, or -*ing* if you can.

ALTERNATIVE HOMEWORK Add endings to your spelling words and write them on the stairs above.

First write all the words going across. Then write those going down. (Not all the words are spelling words.)

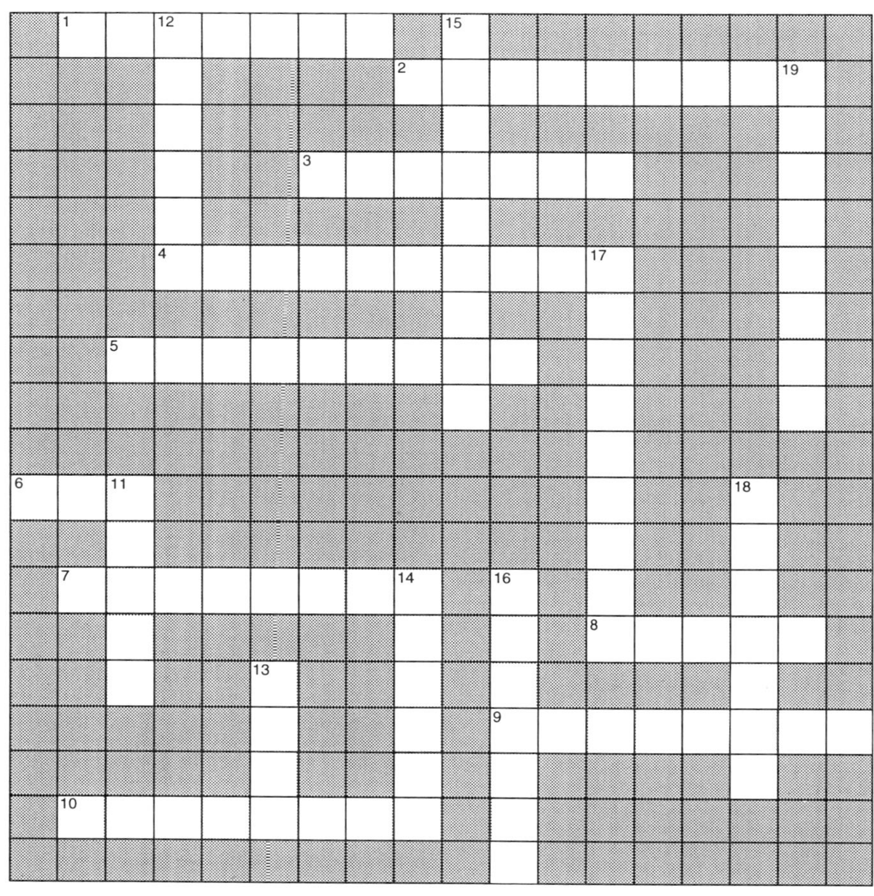

ACROSS

1. A place with many books (Lesson 1)
2. Devices making electric current
3. Young dogs
4. Messiness; carelessness
5. Most sly
6. Opposite of "on"
7. Breeziest
8. Written record of daily events (Lesson 1)
9. The work a person does
10. Answering

DOWN

11. Cooked in hot fat
12. Infants
13. Occupied with many things
14. Making an effort; attempting
15. Joyfulness
16. Things done for fun in spare time
17. Pleased; fulfilled
18. Joined as husband and wife
19. Doing homework

Write the Classroom Words in alphabetical order. ______________________________

______________________________ ______________________________

ALTERNATIVE HOMEWORK Do the activity above or make your own Word Puzzle using your first ten spelling words. Trade puzzles with a classmate.

Copy the words your teacher gives you under Classroom Words. Fold this page back along the dotted line so that only the Pretest column shows. Write the words your teacher dictates.

Spell*well* Words	**Corrections**	**Pretest**
1. brain	____________	1. ____________
2. crayons	____________	2. ____________
3. daisy	____________	3. ____________
4. delay	____________	4. ____________
5. holiday	____________	5. ____________
6. mislaid	____________	6. ____________
7. plainest	____________	7. ____________
8. praise	____________	8. ____________
9. prepaid	____________	9. ____________
10. raisins	____________	10. ____________
11. sprained	____________	11. ____________
12. waist	____________	12. ____________
13. yesterday	____________	13. ____________
Outlaw Word		
14. straight	____________	14. ____________
Classroom Words		
15. ____________	____________	15. ____________
16. ____________	____________	16. ____________
17. ____________	____________	17. ____________
18. ____________	____________	18. ____________

Compare your words with the spelling list. Write the words you did not know in the Corrections column. If all, or all but one, of the words are correct, use the following for your spelling words: **acquaintance, alien, campaign, failure, gaped, mayonnaise,** and **restraint.** Write them in the Corrections column along with the Classroom Words; then do the Alternative Homework this week.

The clock contains many little words. Each is part of a spelling word. Add the missing letters to make a word from this week's list. Then write the whole word on the numbered line.

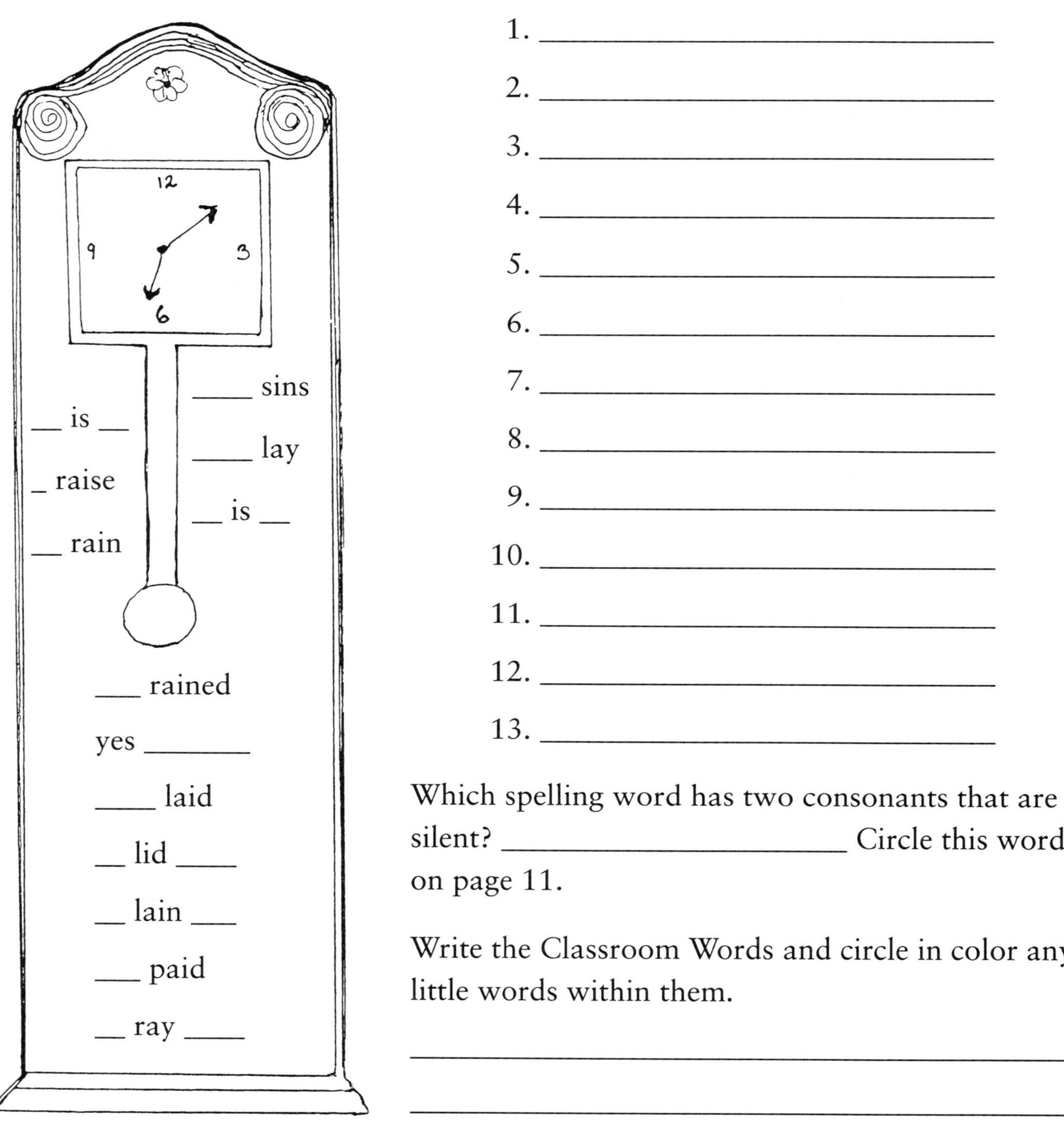

1. ____________________
2. ____________________
3. ____________________
4. ____________________
5. ____________________
6. ____________________
7. ____________________
8. ____________________
9. ____________________
10. ____________________
11. ____________________
12. ____________________
13. ____________________

Which spelling word has two consonants that are silent? ____________________ Circle this word on page 11.

Write the Classroom Words and circle in color any little words within them.

____

____

<u>ALTERNATIVE HOMEWORK</u> In your reading book find 7 words with long *a* that you want to learn. Write them in the Corrections column on page 11. Then write all of your spelling words and their definitions in your personal dictionary.

Write spelling words on the lines below.

SYNONYMS (words that mean the same)

1. postpone ____________________
2. intelligence; the mind ____________________
3. colored, waxed writing tools ____________________
4. injured by a sudden twist ____________________
5. paid beforehand ____________________
6. your middle section ____________________
7. dried grapes ____________________
8. flower with white petals ____________________

ANTONYMS (words that mean the opposite)

9. tomorrow ____________________
10. found ____________________
11. workday ____________________
12. criticize ____________________
13. crooked ____________________
14. fanciest ____________________

Write your Classroom Words followed by their meanings.

____

____

____

____

ALTERNATIVE HOMEWORK How many different words can you make using your spelling words as the root word? If you write fifteen words, you are a whiz! If you think of thirty words, you are a terrific wordmaster!

Fill in the blanks below with spelling words that will make the equations correct.

1. youngster	+	uses ________________	=	solves the puzzle
2. child	+	draws with______________	=	colorful picture
3. bowl of cereal	+	milk and ________________	=	healthy breakfast
4. library book	+	__________________ it	=	overdue book
5. no school or work	+	celebrations	=	________________
6. size 30 pants	+	36-inch ________________	=	pants too small
7. today	–	twenty-four hours	=	________________
8. do not turn left	+	do not turn right	=	go __________ ahead
9. train expected at 8:00	+	half-hour ________________	=	train arrives at 8:30
10. order tickets by mail	+	send check with order	=	________________
11. jogger	+	twisted ankle while running	=	____________ ankle

NOTE: (Choose *ai* or *ay*.) ______ usually comes at the end of a word or syllable. ______ is used in the beginning or middle of a word or syllable.

Now use this rule to make new words. Add *ai* or *ay*.

st______r	gr______n	betr______
cl______	r______nbow	m______lbox
pl______ground	str______	p______nt
subw______	sw______	tr______tor

ALTERNATIVE HOMEWORK Do the activities above.

For this contest you are to find as many words with *ai* as you can. You may use the spelling words. You may ask friends and relatives to help you, and you may use a dictionary. The student with the most correct words is the winner.

1.	____________	16.	____________
2.	____________	17.	____________
3.	____________	18.	____________
4.	____________	19.	____________
5.	____________	20.	____________
6.	____________	21.	____________
7.	____________	22.	____________
8.	____________	23.	____________
9.	____________	24.	____________
10.	____________	25.	____________
11.	____________	26.	____________
12.	____________	27.	____________
13.	____________	28.	____________
14.	____________	29.	____________
15.	____________	30.	____________

Write your Outlaw and Classroom Words in alphabetical order.

____________ ____________

____________ ____________ ____________

ALTERNATIVE HOMEWORK Enter the contest above.

Copy the words your teacher gives you under Classroom Words. Fold this page back along the dotted line so that only the Pretest column shows. Write the words your teacher dictates.

Pretest	Corrections	Spell*well* Words
1. ______	______	1. appear
2. ______	______	2. between
3. ______	______	3. cheerful
4. ______	______	4. disagree
5. ______	______	5. eager
6. ______	______	6. eastern
7. ______	______	7. fearless
8. ______	______	8. freedom
9. ______	______	9. greedy
10. ______	______	10. reason
11. ______	______	11. screamed
12. ______	______	12. speeding
13. ______	______	13. steal
		Outlaw Word
14. ______	______	14. breakfast
		Classroom Words
15. ______	______	15. ______
16. ______	______	16. ______
17. ______	______	17. ______
18. ______	______	18. ______

Compare your words with the spelling list. Write the words you did not know in the Corrections column. If all, or all but one, of the words are correct, use the following for your spelling words: **beacon, bleachers, chimpanzee, committee, defeated, pioneers,** and **sweepstakes.** Write them in the Corrections column along with your Classroom Words; then do the Alternative Homework this week.

Find spelling words that rhyme with the words below. Write these spelling words on the spacecraft; then draw lines to connect the words that rhyme. (Remember: rhymes are not always spelled the same.)

seedy preteen

cheerless weeding

unclear season

fearful meager

dreamed

Write your Outlaw and Classroom Words in color anywhere on the spacecraft.

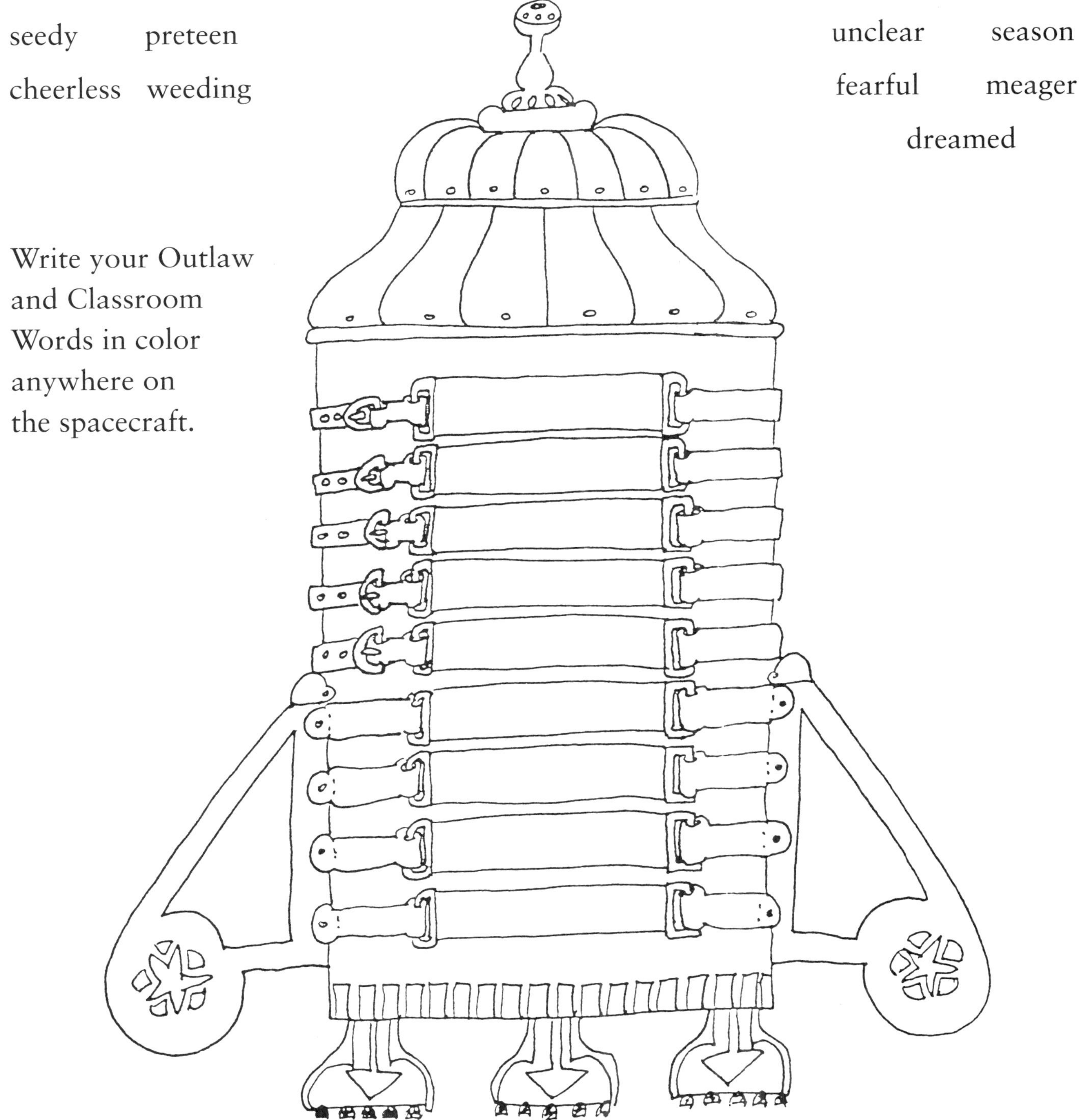

ALTERNATIVE HOMEWORK In your reading book find 7 words with *ee* or *ea* that you want to learn. Write these words in the Corrections column on page 16. Then write all of your spelling words and their definitions in your personal dictionary.

Write the spelling words that answer these questions.

1. Which word gives an explanation?____________________
2. Which word means "to come into view"?____________________
3. Which word describes what robbers do?____________________
4. What is the first meal of the day?____________________
5. Which word describes a section of the country?____________________
6. Which word describes someone very brave?____________________
7. What did the terrified teen do in the haunted house?____________________
8. Which word describes people who want more than they need?____________________
9. Which word describes a friendly, happy person?____________________
10. Which word tells your location when friends sit on both sides of you?____________________
11. Which word tells what friends do when they argue?____________________
12. Which word tells why the American colonies fought England? for____________________
13. Which word describes someone who wants very much to do something?____________________

Write questions like those above using your Classroom Words.

____

____

____

____

<u>ALTERNATIVE HOMEWORK</u> Write a story about an invention you think would be a good idea. Tell its function and how it could be useful to people. Describe what it would look like and what it would be made of.

Add the following prefixes and endings to the words below.

un-

clear
free
real

Write another word with *un-*.

____

dis-

agree
please
appear

Write another word with *dis-*.

____

-ing

scream
steal

Write another word with *-ing*.

____

-y

greed
speed

Write another word with *-y*.

____

-ness

eager
weak
good

Write another word with *-ness*.

____

-ern

east
west
south

Write another word with *-ern*.

____

Add *-ed, -ing, -ful,* and *-less* to the following words:

cheer

fear

Write your Outlaw and Classroom words in capital letters anywhere on this page.

ALTERNATIVE HOMEWORK Add an ending or prefix to each of your spelling words to make new words. Write them in the spaces above. If you cannot add anything, just write the words.

Write a paragraph telling about a trip you would like to take with your family or a friend. Describe the place you would visit; give details about what it looks like and what you would do there.

BOWL-O

Your teacher will dictate all of your spelling words. Write one word on each line of the bowling triangle. If you spell each correctly, you get a strike! Be sure to study any words you misspell, so you can strike it big on tomorrow's test.

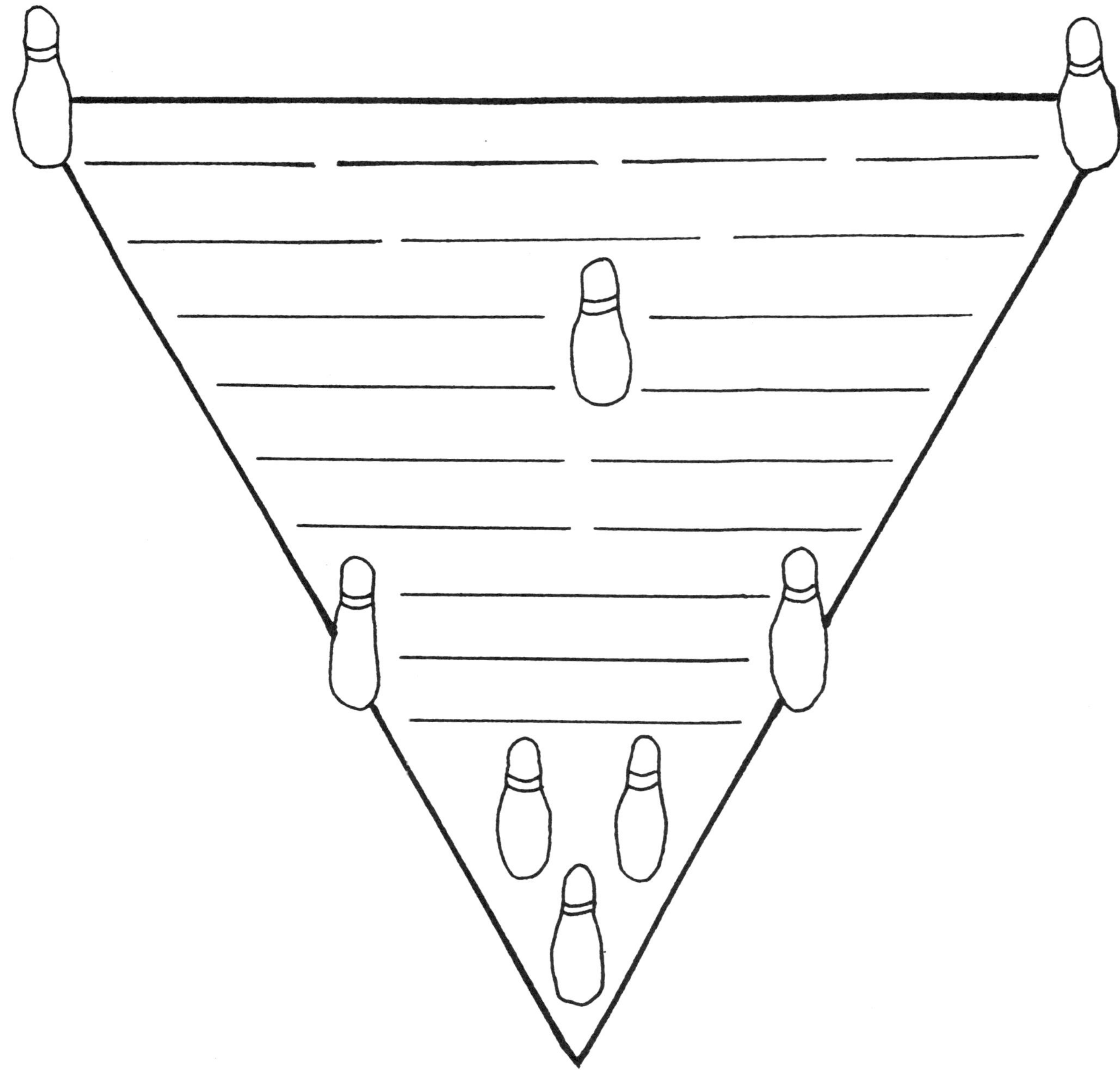

ALTERNATIVE HOMEWORK Do the activities above.

Copy the words your teacher gives you under Classroom Words. Fold this page back along the dotted line so that only the Pretest column shows. Write the words your teacher dictates.

Spell*well* Words	**Corrections**	**Pretest**
1. approach	______________	1. ______________
2. boast	______________	2. ______________
3. following	______________	3. ______________
4. glowed	______________	4. ______________
5. groan	______________	5. ______________
6. hollow	______________	6. ______________
7. loaned	______________	7. ______________
8. owned	______________	8. ______________
9. potato	______________	9. ______________
10. roasting	______________	10. ______________
11. swallow	______________	11. ______________
12. tiptoe	______________	12. ______________
Outlaw Words		
13. double	______________	13. ______________
14. trouble	______________	14. ______________
Classroom Words		
15. ______________	______________	15. ______________
16. ______________	______________	16. ______________
17. ______________	______________	17. ______________
18. ______________	______________	18. ______________

Compare your words with the spelling list. Write the words you did not know in the Corrections column. If all, or all but one, of the words are correct, use the following for your spelling words: **aroma, bungalow, cocoa, locomotive, Olympics, surfboard,** and **uproar.** Write them in the Corrections column along with your Classroom Words; then do the Alternative Homework this week.

Find and circle your spelling words hidden on the computer screen. The words may be horizontal or vertical, but they do *not* overlap. Write the words on the lines below.

x l o a n e d w j h w o t i p t o e b o e n t y u z w r

m b d r o i b l e m n u t g h s x c r i q a z b m z a d

t o a z l d v e m e b o r y a p p r o a c h i o u y t e

a s n a l o l l m v t y o t f s f y p l m k p v t e r l

s g j i o i s w a l l o w u n h y s e d a t t r p m o r

t e r t w b o a s t w t r e n m u o p s w a z d p p u h

n g l o w e d i g h y r e s c g f o l l o w i n g c b o

a b r y u p w s c k b q u i f r o i u r e p l k c s l l

b l p o t a t o n k o s e w m o l u o w n e d t r b e l

c d f v b u i d o u b l e h s a t n i o m g h i w o t o

e s t o a t w e a l e d c b u n r o a s t i n g f c n w

1. ____________________
2. ____________________
3. ____________________
4. ____________________
5. ____________________
6. ____________________
7. ____________________
8. ____________________
9. ____________________
10. ____________________
11. ____________________
12. ____________________
13. ____________________
14. ____________________

Write your Classroom Words in color anywhere on this page.

<u>ALTERNATIVE HOMEWORK</u> In your reading book find 7 words with *oa* or *ow* that you want to learn. Write them in the Corrections column on page 21. Then write all of your spelling words and their definitions in your personal dictionary.

Sometimes words can change meanings the way chameleons change color. Write the correct spelling word for each blank; then circle the meaning the word has in that sentence.

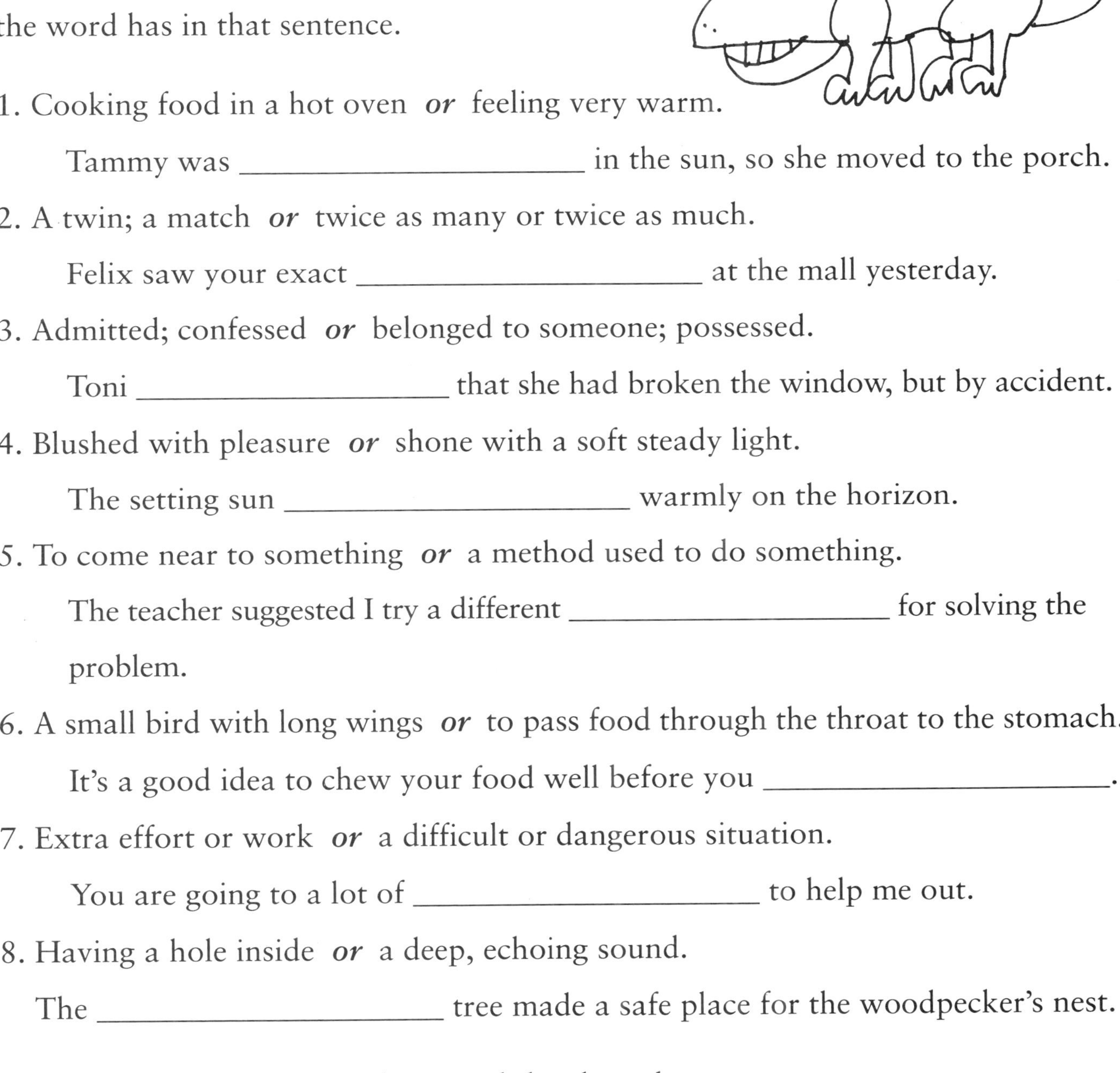

1. Cooking food in a hot oven *or* feeling very warm.

   Tammy was ____________________ in the sun, so she moved to the porch.

2. A twin; a match *or* twice as many or twice as much.

   Felix saw your exact ____________________ at the mall yesterday.

3. Admitted; confessed *or* belonged to someone; possessed.

   Toni ____________________ that she had broken the window, but by accident.

4. Blushed with pleasure *or* shone with a soft steady light.

   The setting sun ____________________ warmly on the horizon.

5. To come near to something *or* a method used to do something.

   The teacher suggested I try a different ____________________ for solving the problem.

6. A small bird with long wings *or* to pass food through the throat to the stomach.

   It's a good idea to chew your food well before you ____________________.

7. Extra effort or work *or* a difficult or dangerous situation.

   You are going to a lot of ____________________ to help me out.

8. Having a hole inside *or* a deep, echoing sound.

   The ____________________ tree made a safe place for the woodpecker's nest.

Write your Classroom Words around the chameleon.

<u>ALTERNATIVE HOMEWORK</u> Choose two of your longest spelling words. Make as many words as possible using these letters. If you write more than twenty words, you are an extraordinary word builder.

Read the headings below. Write one word in each box that fits the category and that starts with the letter at the beginning of the line. (Look at the example.) Use at least *one* spelling word in each category. You may use a dictionary.

	Vegetables	Noises We Can Make	Ways to Walk/Move	Birds	Ways to Help Friends
S		sneeze			
P					
G					
T					
L					

Which word tells that a thing comes near? ____________________

Which word tells what your shadow is doing? ____________________ you.

Which word tells what braggarts do? ____________________

Which words tells what turkeys are doing on holidays? ____________________

Write your Classroom Words and their meanings on the lines below.

____

____

____

____

<u>ALTERNATIVE HOMEWORK</u> Do the activities above.

In this puzzle you will review words from Lessons 1–5. Write the words in the boxes. Then find the secret message by reading the dark boxes going down the page. The numbers tell which lessons the words come from.

1. I hate to listen to Henry _____ about his strength. (5)
2. Renee was ____ when I didn't go to her party. (1)
3. It is ____ of you to eat three pieces of cake. (4)
4. The whole village will be in ____ if the dam breaks. (5)
5. I gave a loud ____ as the doctor moved my sore leg. (5)
6. Turkey and cheese are good ____ two slices of bread. (4)

7. Soon the jet will begin its ____ to the runway. (5)
8. Carla ordered a baked ____ with sour cream. (5)
9. Phil is ____ with me for tomorrow's test. (2)

10. These books are due at the ____ today. (1)
11. The lantern ____ outside our tent. (5)
12. Peanut butter is hard to ____ without water. (5)
13. The Thanksgiving turkey is ____ slowly in the oven. (5)
14. My parents ____ their car for five years before they sold it. (5)

15. The figure skater walked on ____ to protect her blades. (5)
16. The woodchuck ran quickly inside the ____ log. (5)

17. I am sorry, but I am too ____ to baby-sit tonight. (2)
18. Our dog, Ginger, had five ____ last night. (2)
19. The day before today was ____. (3)
20. Since I had to go so far, my friend ____ me his bike. (5)
21. The Milky Way is a ____ of many stars. (1)

22. You fasten your belt around your ____. (3)
23. When you ____ eight, you get sixteen. (5)
24. Knocking over the milk was a ____ thing to do. (1)
25. We are ____ the directions carefully so that we don't get lost. (5)

Write the secret message hidden in the dark boxes. ____________________

____

Do you agree with the message? ____________________

ALTERNATIVE HOMEWORK Do the puzzle above.

Copy the words your teacher gives you under Classroom Words. Fold this page back along the dotted line so that only the Pretest column shows. Write the words your teacher dictates.

Pretest	Corrections	Spell*well* Words
1. ________	________	1. allow
2. ________	________	2. amount
3. ________	________	3. cloudy
4. ________	________	4. crowded
5. ________	________	5. drowsy
6. ________	________	6. frowned
7. ________	________	7. mountain
8. ________	________	8. outdoors
9. ________	________	9. powerful
10. ________	________	10. proud
11. ________	________	11. showers
12. ________	________	12. southeast
13. ________	________	13. thousand
		Outlaw Words
14. ________	________	14. brought
15. ________	________	15. thought
		Classroom Words
16. ________	________	16. ________
17. ________	________	17. ________
18. ________	________	18. ________

Compare your words with the spelling list. Write the words you did not know in the Corrections column. If all, or all but one, of the words are correct, use the following for your spelling words: **blouse, mustache, ounce, pronounce, route, scoundrel, southern,** and **thoughtfully.** Write them in the Corrections column along with your Classroom Words; then do the Alternative Homework this week.

Write your Spell*well* Words under the correct heading. (Notice: both *ou* and *ow* have the sound you say when you hurt yourself.)

ou	*ow*
______________	
______________	______________
______________	______________
______________	______________
______________	______________
______________	______________
______________	______________

Look at the *ow* words. Draw lines between the syllables, and cross out any *-ed* endings. Now finish the rule below.

RULE: Use ________ at the end of a syllable or when followed by a single *n* or *d*.

Write the Classroom Words and circle in color any little words within them.

____

____

Write the smaller word that appears in both Outlaw Words. ______________

ALTERNATIVE HOMEWORK In your reading book find 7 words with *ou* or *ow* that you want to learn. Write them in the Corrections column on page 26. Then write all of your spelling words and their definitions in your personal dictionary.

Read the definitions below. Find the spelling words that fit the meanings and write the syllables in the spaces using a new color for each syllable.

1. Brief rainfalls __ __ __ __ + __ __ __
2. A direction __ __ __ __ __ + __ __ __ __
3. Ready to fall asleep __ __ __ __ + __ __
4. Looked with disapproval __ __ __ __ __ __ __
5. Not indoors __ __ __ + __ __ __ __ __
6. To permit __ __ + __ __ __
7. Not sunny; overcast __ __ __ __ __ + __
8. The total number; the sum __ + __ __ __ __ __
9. Feeling good about what you did __ __ __ __ __
10. Ten one hundreds __ __ __ __ + __ __ __ __
11. Carried or took to a place __ __ __ __ __ __ __
12. Packed or jammed together __ __ __ __ __ + __ __
13. Considered or pictured in one's mind __ __ __ __ __ __ __
14. A high, steep part of the earth __ __ __ __ + __ __ __ __
15. Having great strength __ __ __ + __ __ + __ __ __

Write your Classroom Words in syllables. ______________________________

______________________________ ______________________________

<u>ALTERNATIVE HOMEWORK</u> Write your spelling words in syllables using a different color for each syllable.

Find the spelling word that:

would be on a map of the United States.

____

describes how people feel at a boring show. ____________________

describes a day when there is no sun. ____________________

gives the answer for 20 × 50. ____________________

tells what you could climb in Wyoming or Colorado. ____________________

names what happens on a damp spring day. ____________________

may be written in a math book or checkbook. ____________________

describes the athletes in a weightlifting contest. ____________________

Which spelling word describes:

how your parents feel when you do well? ____________________

what your mom did when she saw your room a mess? ____________________

what your parents do when they give you permission? ____________________

what most students did before answering any questions on a test?

____

where a golf course always is? ____________________

what you did with your school books? ____________________ them to class

Use your Classroom Words to write questions that begin with *what*.

____

____

____

ALTERNATIVE HOMEWORK Make questions using all of your spelling words. Begin some of the questions with *what*. Switch papers with another student and answer each other's questions. Be sure to include a list of the words you used.

For this contest you are to find as many words with *ow* as you can. You may use the spelling words from both Lessons 5 and 6. You may ask friends and relatives to help you, and you may use a dictionary. The student with the most correct words is the winner.

1.	______________	21.	______________
2.	______________	22.	______________
3.	______________	23.	______________
4.	______________	24.	______________
5.	______________	25.	______________
6.	______________	26.	______________
7.	______________	27.	______________
8.	______________	28.	______________
9.	______________	29.	______________
10.	______________	30.	______________
11.	______________	31.	______________
12.	______________	32.	______________
13.	______________	33.	______________
14.	______________	34.	______________
15.	______________	35.	______________
16.	______________	36.	______________
17.	______________	37.	______________
18.	______________	38.	______________
19.	______________	39.	______________
20.	______________	40.	______________

Write your Classroom Words and circle any small words in them in color.

____

____

<u>ALTERNATIVE HOMEWORK</u> Enter the Word-Finder Contest above.

Copy the words your teacher gives you under Classroom Words. Fold this page back along the dotted line so that only the Pretest column shows. Write the words your teacher dictates.

Spell*well* Words	Corrections	Pretest
1. bandage	______	1. ______
2. charge	______	2. ______
3. danger	______	3. ______
4. exchange	______	4. ______
5. garbage	______	5. ______
6. huge	______	6. ______
7. legend	______	7. ______
8. magic	______	8. ______
9. package	______	9. ______
10. passenger	______	10. ______
11. sponge	______	11. ______
12. strange	______	12. ______
Outlaw Words		
13. guess	______	13. ______
14. guide	______	14. ______
Classroom Words		
15. ______	______	15. ______
16. ______	______	16. ______
17. ______	______	17. ______
18. ______	______	18. ______

Compare your words with the spelling list. Write the words you did not know in the Corrections column. If all, or all but one, of the words are correct, use the following for your spelling words: **advantage, beverage, emergency, gymnasium, intelligent, manager,** and **rigid.** Write them in the Corrections column along with your Classroom Words; then do the Alternative Homework this week.

The clock contains many little words. Each is part of a spelling word. Add the missing letters to make a word from this week's list. Then write the whole word on the numbered line.

hug ___
magi __
__ ran ____
band______
___ on _____
char_______
____hang__
pass_______
pack ______
______ anger
garb_______
leg_________

1. ______________________
2. ______________________
3. ______________________
4. ______________________
5. ______________________
6. ______________________
7. ______________________
8. ______________________
9. ______________________
10. ______________________
11. ______________________
12. ______________________

Write the Classroom Words; circle in color any little words within them.

____

____

Which spelling words were not used on this page?

______________________ ______________________

ALTERNATIVE HOMEWORK In your reading book find 7 words that you want to learn. Write these words in the Corrections column on page 31. Then write all of your spelling words and their definitions in your personal dictionary.

Write spelling words on the lines below.

SYNONYMS (words that mean the same)

1. a parcel or bundle ______________________
2. a rider on a train or bus ______________________
3. wizardry or witchcraft ______________________
4. trade for something else ______________________
5. an old story or myth ______________________
6. a thick pad to soak up spills ______________________
7. to cover a wound ______________________
8. rush forward ______________________

ANTONYMS (words that mean the opposite)

9. tiny ______________________
10. safety ______________________
11. follower ______________________
12. certain; sure ______________________
13. regular; familiar ______________________

Look at the spelling words as well as the Alternate Words on page 31.

RULE: When *g* is followed by the letters: ___, ___, or ___, the *g* usually sounds like /j/.

Look at the Outlaw Words. Why do they have *u* after *g*? ____________

Write four questions, using each of your Classroom Words.

____

____

____

____

ALTERNATIVE HOMEWORK Write synonyms or antonyms for eight of your spelling words. Trade papers with a classmate and work each other's puzzle.

Write as many words as you can that use the following prefix and ending. Be sure to include the Spell*well* Words.

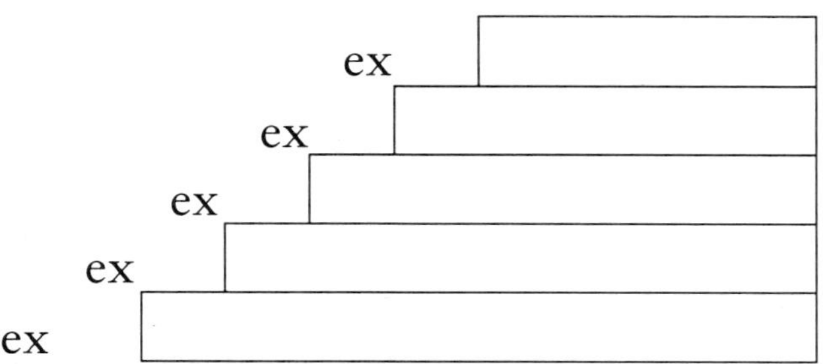

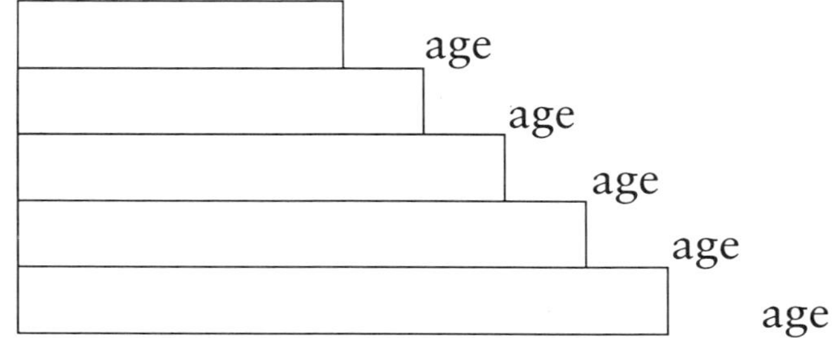

Add *-est* to two spelling words. Then write another word that is not on the spelling list.

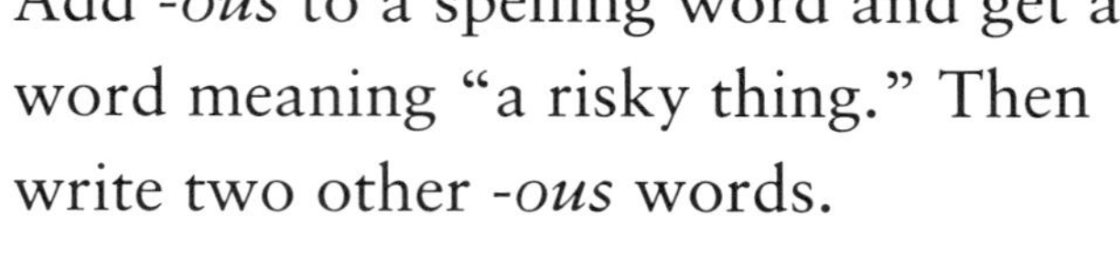

Add *-ous* to a spelling word and get a word meaning "a risky thing." Then write two other *-ous* words.

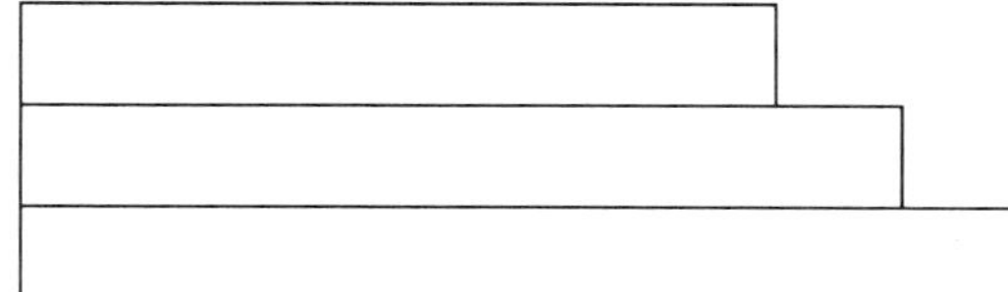

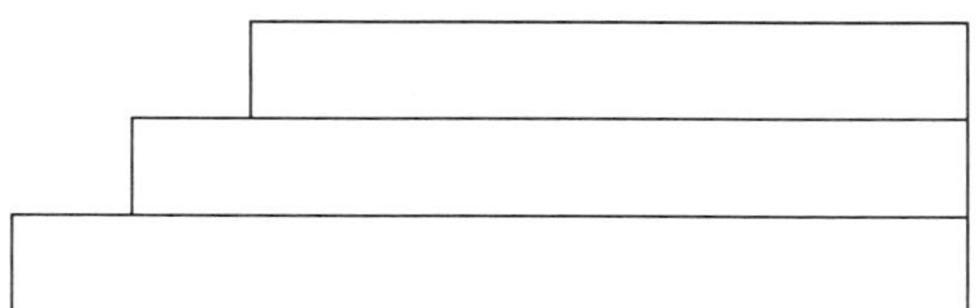

Add *-ing* to seven spelling words. Don't forget the Outlaw Words!

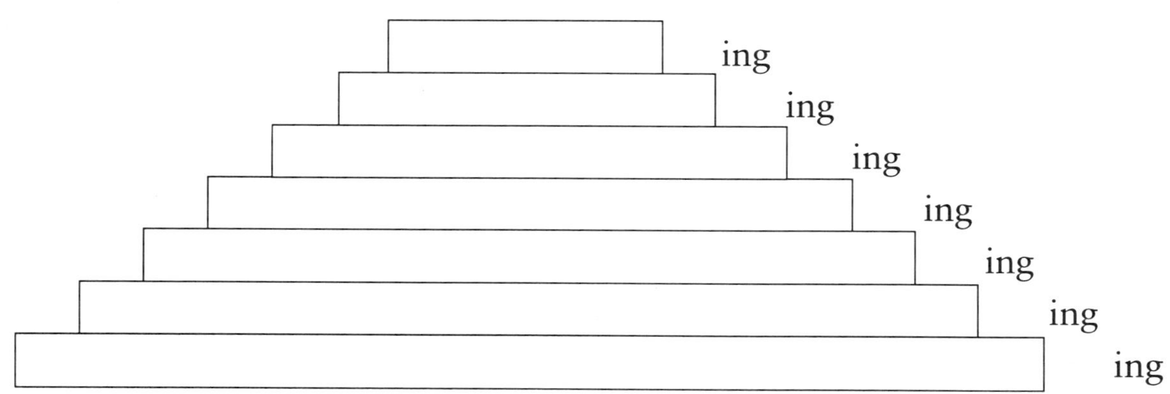

Write the Spell*well* Words that *end* with the third and fourth letters of the alphabet. ____

<u>ALTERNATIVE HOMEWORK</u> Imagine a class where the teacher becomes drowsy. Write a story that tells why the teacher is sleepy and what happens in the class because of this.

Imagine that you and a friend are in danger. Write a story telling what the danger is and how you escape. Use some spelling words in your story.

ARCHERY PRACTICE

Write each spelling word your teacher dictates in the space with the correct beginning letter and the right number of blanks.

g _ _ _ _ _ _

e _ _ _ _ _ _ _

g _ _ _ _

p _ _ _ _ _ _

h _ _ _

b _ _ _ _ _ _

s _ _ _ _ _

m _ _ _ _

l _ _ _ _ _

c _ _ _ _ _

g _ _ _ _

s _ _ _ _ _ _

d _ _ _ _ _

p _ _ _ _ _ _ _ _

Write your Classroom Words in color anywhere on this page.

<u>ALTERNATIVE HOMEWORK</u> Do both activities above.

Copy the words your teacher gives you under Classroom Words. Fold this page back along the dotted line so that only the Pretest column shows. Write the words your teacher dictates.

Pretest	Corrections	Spell*well* Words
1. ______	______	1. advice
2. ______	______	2. bicycle
3. ______	______	3. center
4. ______	______	4. chance
5. ______	______	5. circle
6. ______	______	6. decide
7. ______	______	7. exciting
8. ______	______	8. fancy
9. ______	______	9. force
10. ______	______	10. price
11. ______	______	11. recess
12. ______	______	12. sentence
		Outlaw Words
13. ______	______	13. juice
14. ______	______	14. ocean
15. ______	______	15. practice
		Classroom Words
16. ______	______	16. ______
17. ______	______	17. ______
18. ______	______	18. ______

Compare your words with the spelling list. Write the words you did not know in the Corrections column. If all, or all but one, of the words are correct, use the following for your spelling words: **accomplice, bounce, celebrity, celery, circulation, medicine,** and **recipe.** Write them in the Corrections column along with the Classroom Words; then do the Alternative Homework this week.

Find spelling words that rhyme with the words below. Write these spelling words on the spacecraft; then draw lines connecting the words that rhyme. (Watch out! Rhymes are not always spelled the same.)

dance notion

Nancy renter

refried

horse twice

moose depress

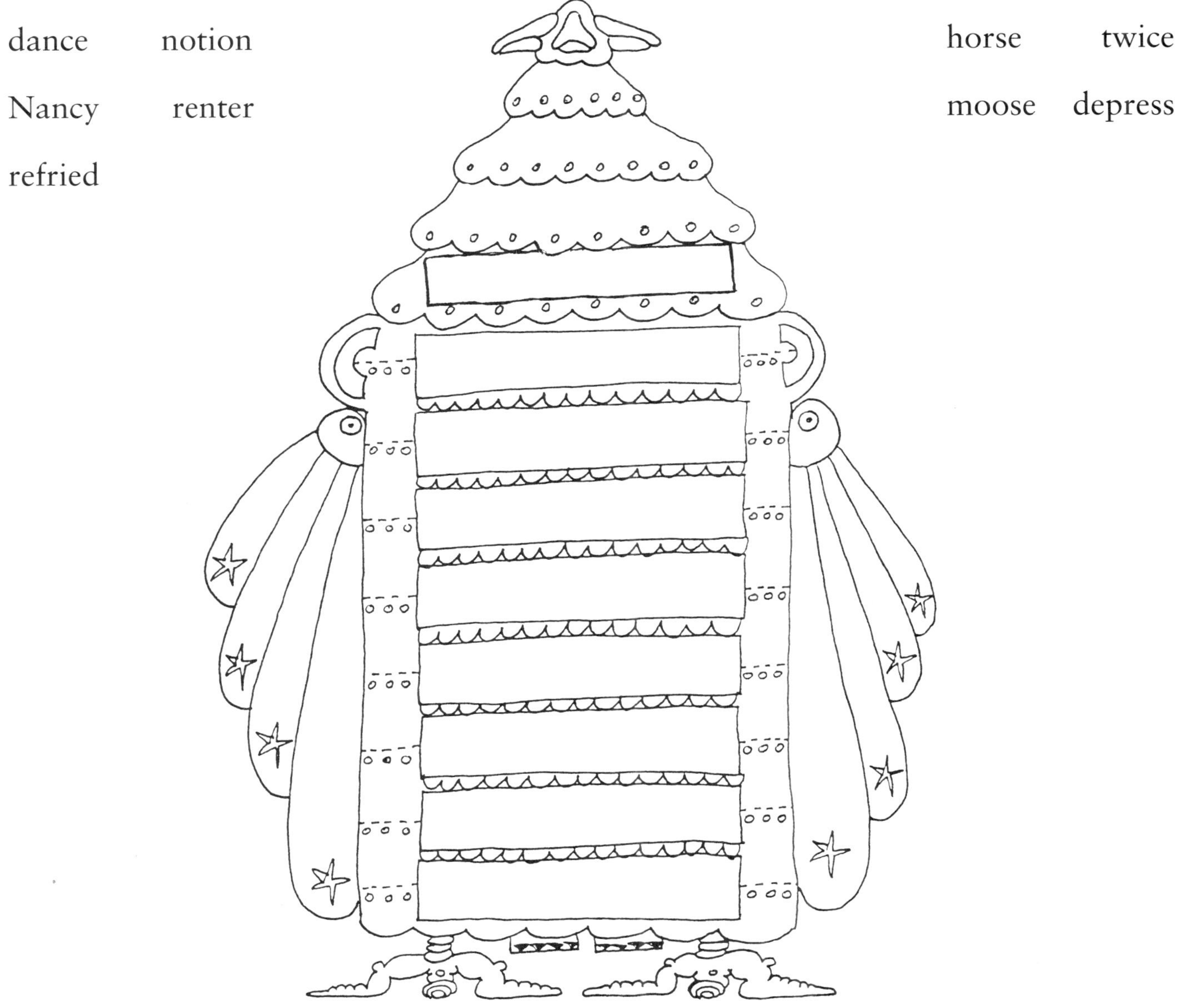

Write your Classroom Words in alphabetical order. ______________________________

______________________________ ______________________________

ALTERNATIVE HOMEWORK In your reading book find 8 words with two or more syllables that you want to learn. Write these words in the Corrections column on page 36. Then write all of your spelling words and their definitions in your personal dictionary.

Write the spelling words that answer these questions.

1. Which spelling word names a round shape? ________________
2. Which word names the free time at school? ________________
3. Which spelling word tells the cost of something? ______________
4. Which word tells what you must do to skate well? ____________________
5. Which word means luck or an unpredictable event? ____________________
6. Which spelling word describes the middle of a circle? ____________________
7. Which word names a vehicle with only two wheels? ____________________
8. Which word describes a thrilling story or movie? ____________________
9. Which word tells what you need to open a jammed door? __________________
10. Which word tells what you give a friend who asks for your opinion? ____________________
11. Which word describes a crown covered with jewels? ____________________
12. Which names a group of words with a subject and verb? __________________
13. Which word tells what you do when you make up your mind? ____________________

Look at the words. What sound does the *c* in these spelling words make? _____

RULE: When *c* is followed by ___, ___, or ___, the *c* says ______.

Write the spelling words that were **not** used on this page in the margin.

<u>ALTERNATIVE HOMEWORK</u> Write questions like those above using the Classroom Words and eight other words from your spelling list. Exchange papers with a classmate and write the answers. Be sure to include your individual spelling list.

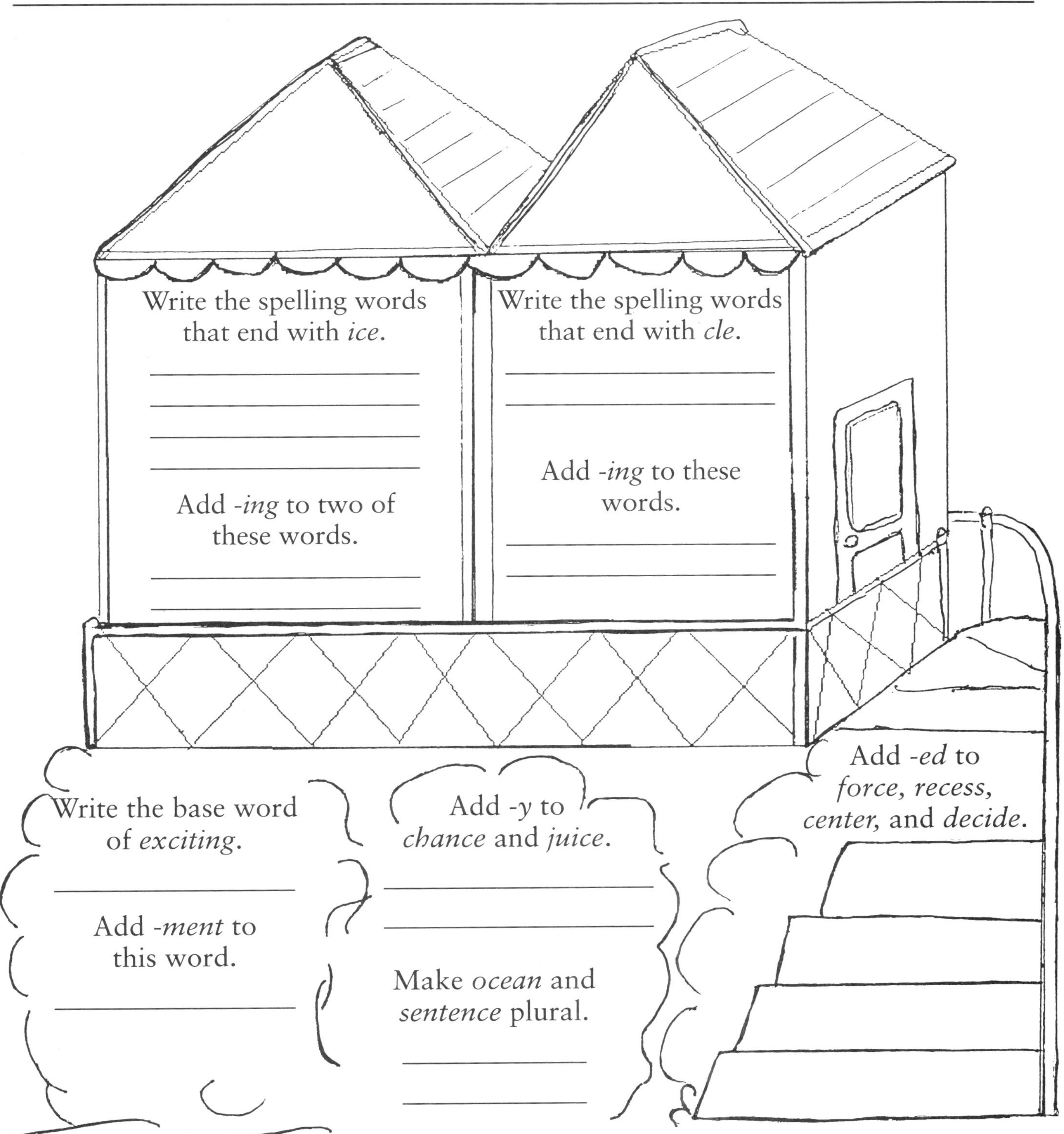

Write your Classroom Words in color on the roof.

ALTERNATIVE HOMEWORK Add any endings or prefixes to your spelling words, and write them on the lines above. If you cannot add anything, just write the words.

Write a paragraph about what you do at recess. Describe several things. Tell which ones you like the most and why. How do these change as the seasons change?

BOWL-O

Your teacher will dictate all of your spelling words. Write one word on each line of the bowling triangle. If you spell each correctly, you get a strike! Be sure to study any words you misspell, so you can strike it big on tomorrow's test.

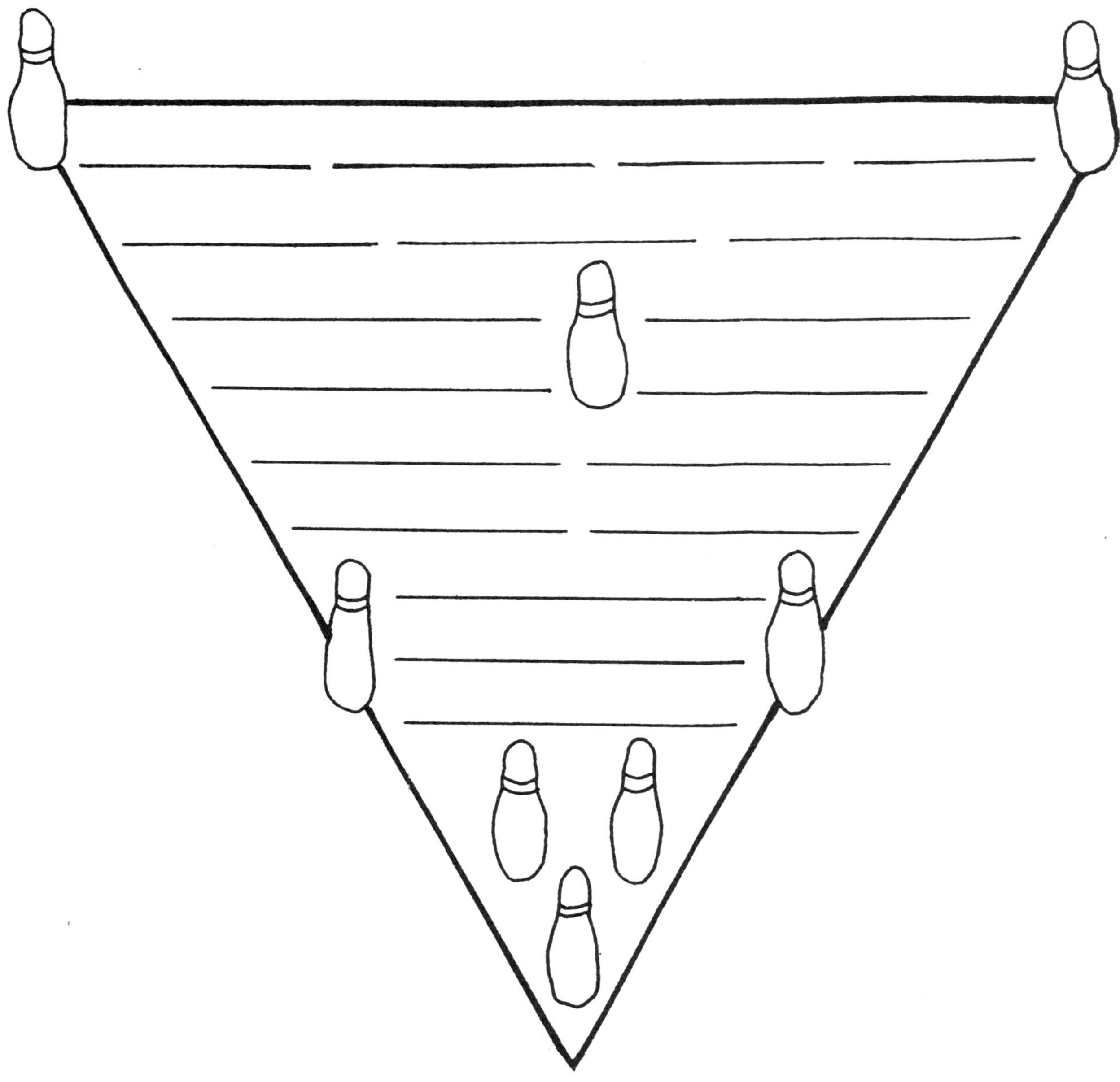

ALTERNATIVE HOMEWORK Do the activities above.

Copy the words your teacher gives you under Classroom Words. Fold this page back along the dotted line so that only the Pretest column shows. Write the words your teacher dictates.

Spell*well* Words	Corrections	Pretest
1. avoid	______	1. ______
2. broiled	______	2. ______
3. choice	______	3. ______
4. destroy	______	4. ______
5. disappoint	______	5. ______
6. employ	______	6. ______
7. enjoyed	______	7. ______
8. noise	______	8. ______
9. poison	______	9. ______
10. royalty	______	10. ______
11. soybeans	______	11. ______
12. voice	______	12. ______
Outlaw Words		
13. laugh	______	13. ______
14. laughter	______	14. ______
Classroom Words		
15. ______	______	15. ______
16. ______	______	16. ______
17. ______	______	17. ______
18. ______	______	18. ______

Compare your words with the spelling list. Write the words you did not know in the Corrections column. If all, or all but one, of the words are correct, use the following for your spelling words: **adjoining, appointment, boycott, coyote, embroider, hoisting,** and **loitered.** Write them in the Corrections column along with your Classroom Words; then do the Alternative Homework this week.

Underline any endings on your spelling words on page 41. Next write all the words under the correct heading. Then add another word that fits each pattern on the line marked with the *.

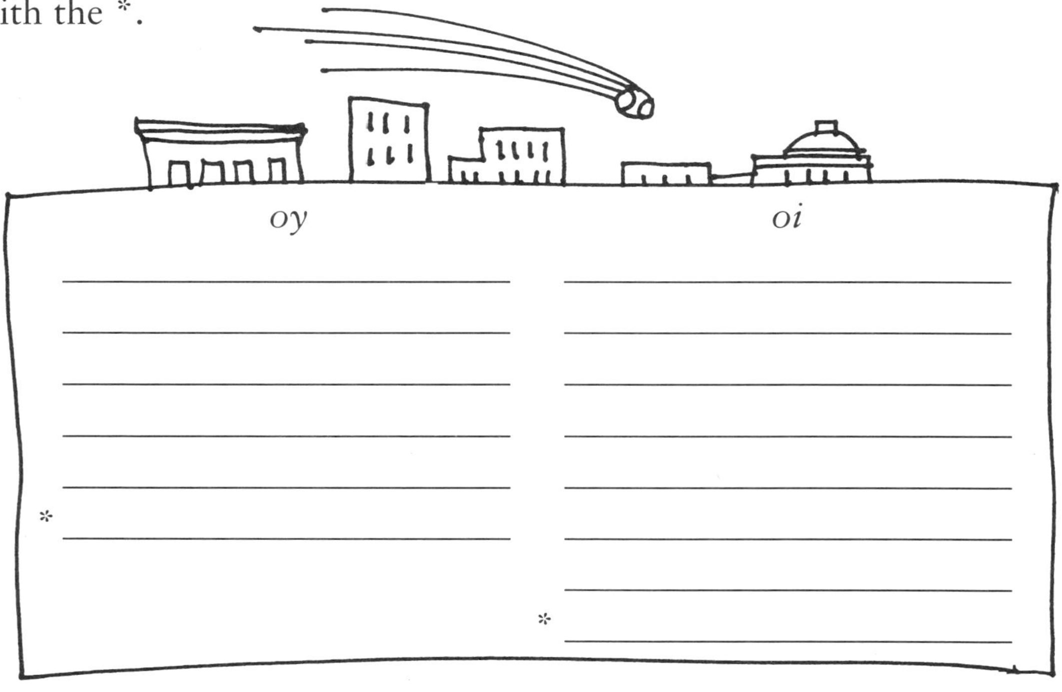

NOTICE: *Oi* and *oy* both have the same sound. Which do you use at the end of a word or syllable? ____________

Which do you use in the middle of a word? ____________ Now write the rule.

RULE: Use *oy* at the ______ of a word or syllable, but use *oi* in the _________.

Add *oi* or *oy* to the words below. (Don't forget the rule!)

m_____st	j_____n	sp_____l
embr_____der	b_____ling	c_____l
f_____l	empl_____	cowb_____

Write the Outlaw Words in sentences. Circle the vowels.

____

____

Write your Classroom Words in color anywhere on this page.

ALTERNATIVE HOMEWORK In your reading book find 7 words you want to learn. Write them in the Corrections column on page 41. Then write all of your spelling words and their definitions in your personal dictionary.

Sometimes words can change meanings the way chameleons change color. Write the correct spelling word for each blank; then circle the meaning the word has in that sentence.

1. Had a good time *or* had as an advantage.

   Deena ____________________ a comfortable lead for the entire race.

2. To keep from happening *or* to stay away from.

   If I return the library books on time, I'll _______________ paying a fine.

3. Became very hot or overly warm *or* cooked over an open flame.

   We __________________ with our coats on at noon in the hot sun.

4. The chance to choose *or* excellent quality; preferred above others.

   Sometimes it's hard to make a ____________________ at the video store.

5. Something that harms or kills *or* to have a bad effect on.

   Gossip can __________________ the minds of other people with lies.

6. Hire and then put to work *or* make use of.

   That new factory will ____________________two hundred workers.

7. Any sound *or* an unpleasant, loud commotion.

   Mother told my friends and me to keep the ____________________ down.

8. The sound produced through the mouth *or* to express or utter.

   We all have a right to ____________________ our opinions.

Write your Outlaw and Classroom Words; then circle in color any little words you see in them.

____

____

____

ALTERNATIVE HOMEWORK Write questions using ten of your spelling words and beginning with the word *when*. Exchange papers with another student and answer each other's questions.

Fill in the blanks below with spelling words that will make the equations correct.

1. raw beef	+	________________	=	grilled steak
2. tickets to game	+	game canceled	=	________________ed fans
3. sore throat	+	lost ______________	=	can't talk on phone
4. kings and queens	+	princes and princesses	=	______________________
5. home alone	+	hear loud __________	=	startled and scared
6. weak building	+	severe hurricane	=	building _____________ed
7. zoo	+	monkeys doing tricks	=	make children ___________
8. select a book	+	enjoy reading it	=	good __________________
9. insect pests	+	destroying crops	=	farmer uses ____________
10. birthday party	+	a lot of laughter	=	___________ the celebration
11. ______________	+	processed into squares	=	tofu
12. see poison ivy	+	walk around it	=	______________ touching it

Write your Outlaw and Classroom Words in sentences.

____

____

____

____

____

____

<u>ALTERNATIVE HOMEWORK</u> How many different words can you make using your spelling words as the root or base word? If you write fifteen words, you are a whiz! If you think of thirty words, you are a terrific wordmaster!

For this contest you are to find as many words with *oi* and *oy* as you can. You may use the spelling words. You may ask friends and relatives to help you, and you may use a dictionary. The student with the most correct words is the winner.

1. ______________________
2. ______________________
3. ______________________
4. ______________________
5. ______________________
6. ______________________
7. ______________________
8. ______________________
9. ______________________
10. ______________________
11. ______________________
12. ______________________
13. ______________________
14. ______________________
15. ______________________
16. ______________________
17. ______________________
18. ______________________
19. ______________________
20. ______________________
21. ______________________
22. ______________________
23. ______________________
24. ______________________
25. ______________________
26. ______________________
27. ______________________
28. ______________________
29. ______________________
30. ______________________
31. ______________________
32. ______________________
33. ______________________
34. ______________________
35. ______________________
36. ______________________
37. ______________________
38. ______________________
39. ______________________
40. ______________________

Write your Outlaw and Classroom Words beginning with the longest word and ending with the shortest.

____

____

____

ALTERNATIVE HOMEWORK Enter the Word-Finder Contest above.

Copy the words your teacher gives you under Classroom Words. Fold this page back along the dotted line so that only the Pretest column shows. Write the words your teacher dictates.

Pretest	Corrections	Spell*well* Words
1. ______	______	1. **astronaut**
2. ______	______	2. **August**
3. ______	______	3. **author**
4. ______	______	4. **autograph**
5. ______	______	5. **automatic**
6. ______	______	6. **awful**
7. ______	______	7. **cause**
8. ______	______	8. **crawled**
9. ______	______	9. **fault**
10. ______	______	10. **haunted**
11. ______	______	11. **straws**
12. ______	______	12. **yawning**
		Outlaw Words
13. ______	______	13. **caught**
14. ______	______	14. **daughter**
		Classroom Words
15. ______	______	15. ______
16. ______	______	16. ______
17. ______	______	17. ______
18. ______	______	18. ______

Compare your words with the spelling list. Write the words you did not know in the Corrections column. If all, or all but one, of the words are correct, use the following for your spelling words: **brawl, gauge, Hawaii, lawyer, saucer, sprawled,** and **tomahawk.** Write them in the Corrections column along with your Classroom Words; then do the Alternative Homework this week.

Circle the endings of these words. Write the root or base word below.

yawning autographed crawling haunted

__________ __________ __________ __________

Circle the *-ly* and write the root below.

awfully awkwardly

__________ __________

Now circle the prefix at the beginning of each word. Notice that the root is at the *end* of the word. Write the roots below.

autograph telegraph phonograph

__________ __________ __________

In each word this root means "written."

If the prefix *auto* means "self," what do these words mean?

autograph ______________________________

automatic ______________________________

autobiography ______________________________

automobile ______________________________

Circle the prefixes at the beginning of these words.
Write the root or base word below.

default because uncaught stepdaughter

__________ __________ __________ __________

Write three spelling words that name people. ____________________

____________________ ____________________

ALTERNATIVE HOMEWORK In your reading book find 7 words that you want to learn. Write them in the Corrections column on page 46. Then write all of your spelling words and their definitions in your personal dictionary.

Write spelling words on the lines below.

SYNONYMS (words that mean the same)

1. a writer ____________________
2. signature ____________________
3. crept along ____________________
4. tubes for sipping ____________________
5. the eighth month ____________________
6. a space traveler ____________________
7. operating by itself ____________________
8. inhabited by ghosts ____________________
9. opening the mouth wide for more air ____________________

ANTONYMS (words that mean the opposite)

10. son ____________________
11. result ____________________
12. freed or released ____________________
13. wonderful ____________________
14. no blame ____________________

Write four sentences using your Classroom Words.

____

____

____

____

ALTERNATIVE HOMEWORK Write synonyms or antonyms for your spelling words. Trade papers with a friend and write the answers for each other's words.

Which spelling word tells who or what you would find:

on a calendar? ________________

in outer space? ________________

brought with your milkshake? ________________

writing at a desk or a word processor? ________________

Which spelling word tells:

about a house that a ghost lives in? ________________

what your mother is to your grandmother? ________________

what you might find yourself doing if you're bored? ________________

what you did when you were a baby? ________________

how you feel when you are sick? ________________

what you did to the mouse in your house? ________________

what you say when you didn't do it? "It's not my ________________."

what we say when we ask why something happened?

"What was the ________________?"

Which word describes a machine that operates by itself? ________________

Write your Classroom Words beginning with the longest and ending with the shortest.

____

____

<u>ALTERNATIVE HOMEWORK</u> Write a letter to your parents asking them to change one rule at home that you do not like. Include at least three reasons why you would like to have this rule changed.

Write a paragraph about a famous person. Tell why this person is well-known. What did he or she do? Why are you interested in him or her? Would you want to be this person? Why or why not? Use at least five spelling words in your paragraph.

ARCHERY PRACTICE

Write each spelling word your teacher dictates in the space with the correct beginning letter and the right number of blanks.

Now write the Classroom Words around the outside of the target as your teacher dictates them.

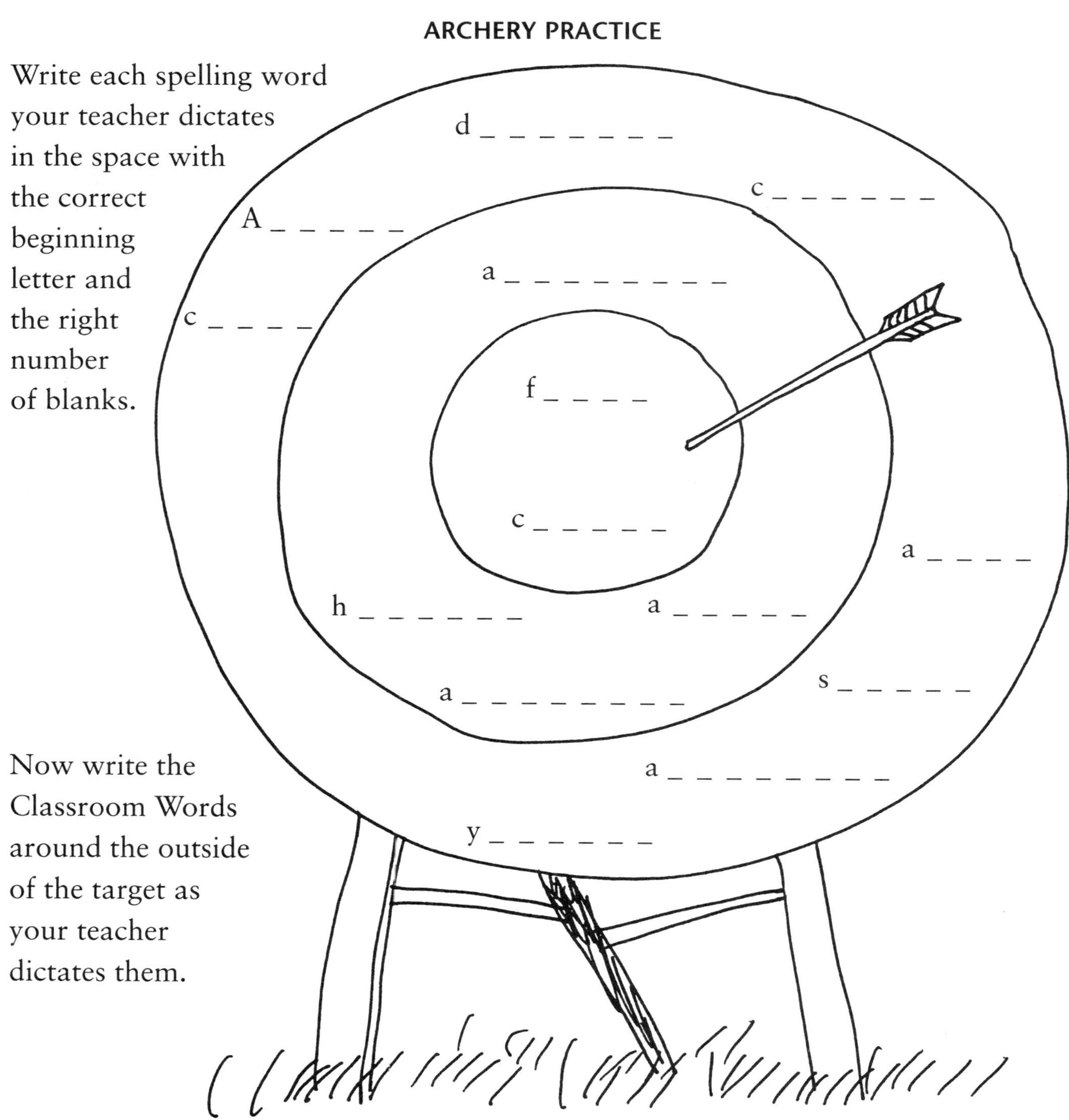

Be sure to study your spelling words for the test tomorrow!

<u>ALTERNATIVE HOMEWORK</u> Do both activities above.

Copy the words your teacher gives you under Classroom Words. Fold this page back along the dotted line so that only the Pretest column shows. Write the words your teacher dictates.

Spell*well* Words	Corrections	Pretest
1. **believe**	______	1. ______
2. **brief**	______	2. ______
3. **ceiling**	______	3. ______
4. **chiefly**	______	4. ______
5. **eighteen**	______	5. ______
6. **field**	______	6. ______
7. **neighbor**	______	7. ______
8. **receive**	______	8. ______
9. **reindeer**	______	9. ______
10. **relief**	______	10. ______
11. **thief**	______	11. ______
12. **weigh**	______	12. ______
Outlaw Words		
13. **either**	______	13. ______
14. **neither**	______	14. ______
Classroom Words		
15. ______	______	15. ______
16. ______	______	16. ______
17. ______	______	17. ______
18. ______	______	18. ______

Compare your words with the spelling list. Write the words you did not know in the Corrections column. If all, or all but one, of the words are correct, use the following for your spelling words: **chieftain, deceive, freight, grieving, pierce, seize,** and **shriek.** Write them in the Corrections column along with the Classroom Words; then do the Alternative Homework this week.

Write your Spell*well* Words under the correct headings.

sound of /ē/—spelled *ie*

____
____
____
____
____
____

sound of /ā/—spelled *ei*

____
____
____
____

sound of /ē/—spelled *ei*

____
____

Circle the letter that comes before *ei* in these words. Write it: ______________

RULE: *i* comes before *e*, except after ____, or when sounded like /ā/.

Write your Outlaw and Classroom Words in color in alphabetical order.

______________________ ______________________
______________________ ______________________
______________________ ______________________

<u>ALTERNATIVE HOMEWORK</u> In your reading book find 7 words that you want to learn. Write them in the Corrections column on page 51. Then write all of your spelling words and their definitions in your personal dictionary.

Write the spelling words that answer these questions.

1. Which word names an animal?____________________
2. Which word tells a number?____________________
3. Which word names a criminal?____________________
4. Which word means "one or the other"?____________________
5. Which word means "short in time"?____________________
6. Which word means "mainly; mostly"?____________________
7. Which word tells a place to play ball?____________________
8. Which word tells what you feel when a pain stops?____________________
9. Which word tells what a doctor's scale can do?____________________
10. Which word names someone living nearby?____________________
11. Which word names the top of the room?____________________
12. Which word means "to accept as true"?____________________

Write questions using the six spelling words that were **not** used on this page. Begin with *why*. Exchange papers with a classmate; answer each other's questions.

____

____

____

____

____

____

____

<u>ALTERNATIVE HOMEWORK</u> Write a paragraph that tells how you *feel* about school vacation. Tell why you feel this way and how you show it. Include where you like to spend your vacation and what you like to do there. Don't forget to begin with a topic sentence.

Read the headings below. Write one word in each box that fits the category and that starts with the letter at the beginning of the line. (Look at the example.) Use at least one spelling word in each category. You may use a dictionary.

	Feelings	Animals and Birds	Sports Terms	Words That Name People	Parts of a Building
F					
N	numbness				
R					
T					
C					

Write your Classroom Words with their meanings.

____

____

____

____

ALTERNATIVE HOMEWORK Do the activity above.

First write all the words across. Then write those going down. (The words are from this week's lesson, except where noted.)

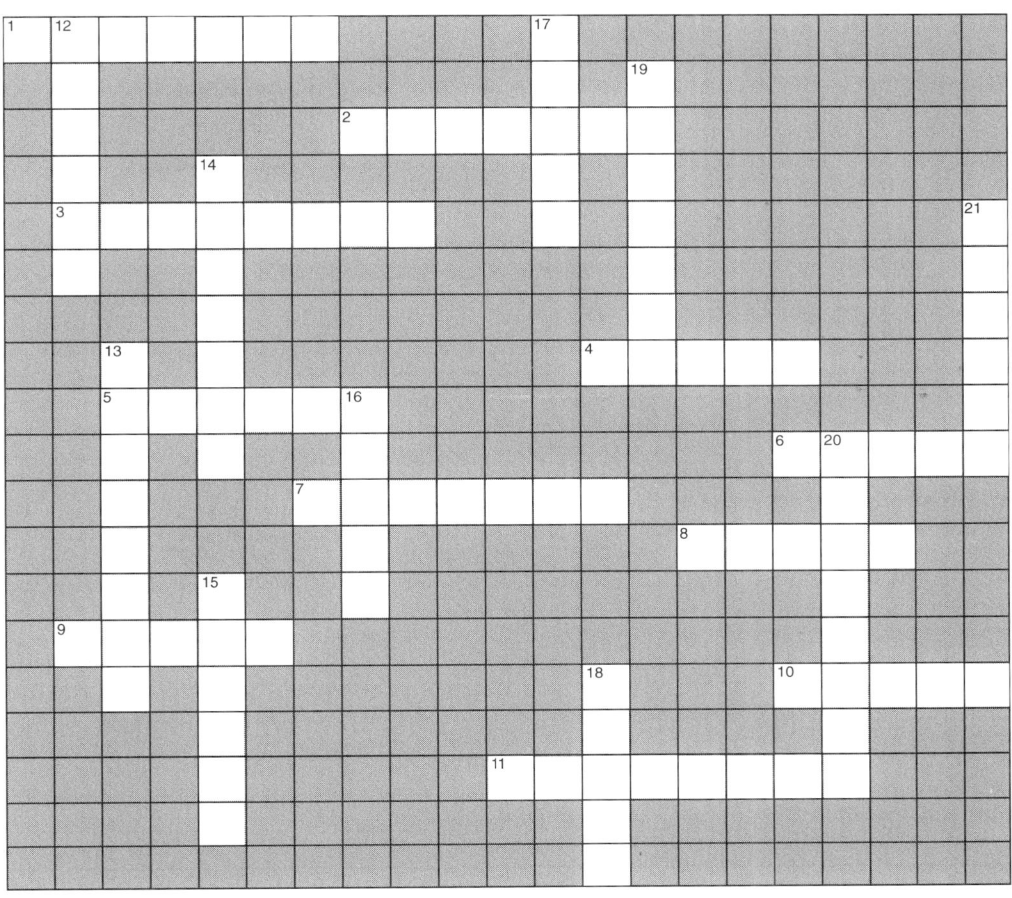

ACROSS

1. To think something is true
2. To take or accept
3. One and a half dozen
4. Very short in length
5. A comfort or a help
6. The cost of something (Lesson 8)
7. Upper surface of the room
8. Stay clear of or away from (Lesson 9)
9. A large body of water (Lesson 8)
10. To put on a scale
11. A person who lives next door

DOWN

12. One or the other
13. To do something over and over to get better (Lesson 8)
14. Most importantly
15. Hooked or trapped (Lesson 10)
16. An open space of land
17. A loud sound (Lesson 9)
18. A robber
19. Not either one
20. A large animal with antlers
21. The act of choosing (Lesson 9)

Write the Classroom Words in the margins.

ALTERNATIVE HOMEWORK Using your first eight spelling words, write a puzzle like the one above. Exchange papers with a classmate and fill in the correct words.

Copy the words your teacher gives you under Classroom Words. Fold this page back along the dotted line so that only the Pretest column shows. Write the words your teacher dictates.

Pretest	Corrections	Spell*well* Words
1. ________	________	1. castle
2. ________	________	2. ghost
3. ________	________	3. honest
4. ________	________	4. hours
5. ________	________	5. knee
6. ________	________	6. knife
7. ________	________	7. knight
8. ________	________	8. knot
9. ________	________	9. thumb
10. ________	________	10. whistle
11. ________	________	11. wreck
12. ________	________	12. wrestle
13. ________	________	13. wrist
		Outlaw Word
14. ________	________	14. often
		Classroom Words
15. ________	________	15. ________
16. ________	________	16. ________
17. ________	________	17. ________
18. ________	________	18. ________

Compare your words with the spelling list. Write the words you did not know in the Corrections column. If all, or all but one, of the words are correct, use the following for your spelling words: **cupboard, herbs, honeycomb, honorable, knowledge, salmon,** and **wreath.** Write them in the Corrections column along with your Classroom Words; then do the Alternative Homework this week.

Find and circle the spelling words hidden on the computer screen. The words may be horizontal or vertical, but they do *not* overlap. Write the words on the lines below.

```
a c w r e s t l e n a t e p g t o s t f x h o u r s t
d o d n h o n e s t a i n o d o e k a a g n o p m e c
i n p c a s t l e g a r w r e c k p s b o l o f t e n
m b l k n i f e o h d e h i i n u e r d s t r t k r m
o t l r a f f u t o e o o a t e s l i v y a t v n b j
k n i g h t a k u s t r i m o a p w r i s t h k e t y
h m o i s e a n o t p a t m y c t t c v s v o p e h r
n a u g i n g o d r e n t y o n s t h u m b m s k x y
l c a r f e x t l n c k a b r w h i s t l e b r p n g
```

1. ______ 8. ______

2. ______ 9. ______

3. ______ 10. ______

4. ______ 11. ______

5. ______ 12. ______

6. ______ 13. ______

7. ______ 14. ______

Write your Classroom Words in alphabetical order.

______

______

ALTERNATIVE HOMEWORK In your reading book find 7 words that you want to learn. Write them in the Corrections column on page 56. Then write all your spelling words and their definitions in your personal dictionary.

Write the spelling words on the lines below.

SYNONYMS (words that mean the same)

1. leg joint ____________________
2. a cutting blade ____________________
3. to fight or struggle ____________________
4. phantom; spook ____________________
5. a tangle of yarn or line ____________________
6. medieval soldier ____________________
7. 60-minute periods ____________________
8. a shrill sound or birdcall ____________________

ANTONYMS (words that mean the opposite)

9. shack ____________________
10. build ____________________
11. infrequently ____________________
12. lying; deceitful ____________________

Write the two Spell*well* Words you did not use above.

____

Write four questions using your Classroom Words.

____

____

____

____

<u>ALTERNATIVE HOMEWORK</u> Write a story about a magic cupboard. Tell why it is magic, what you find in it, and what you will do about it. Try to use some other spelling words in your story.

ALTERNATIVE HOMEWORK How many different words can you make using your spelling words as the root or base word? If you write twenty-five words, you are a whiz! If you think of fifty words, you are a champion wordmaster!

Write an adventure story that involves a knight, a castle, and a knife. Be sure to include interesting details about each.

BOWL-O

Your teacher will dictate all of your spelling words. Write one word on each line of the bowling triangle. If you spell each correctly, you get a strike! Be sure to study any words you misspell, so you can strike it big on tomorrow's test.

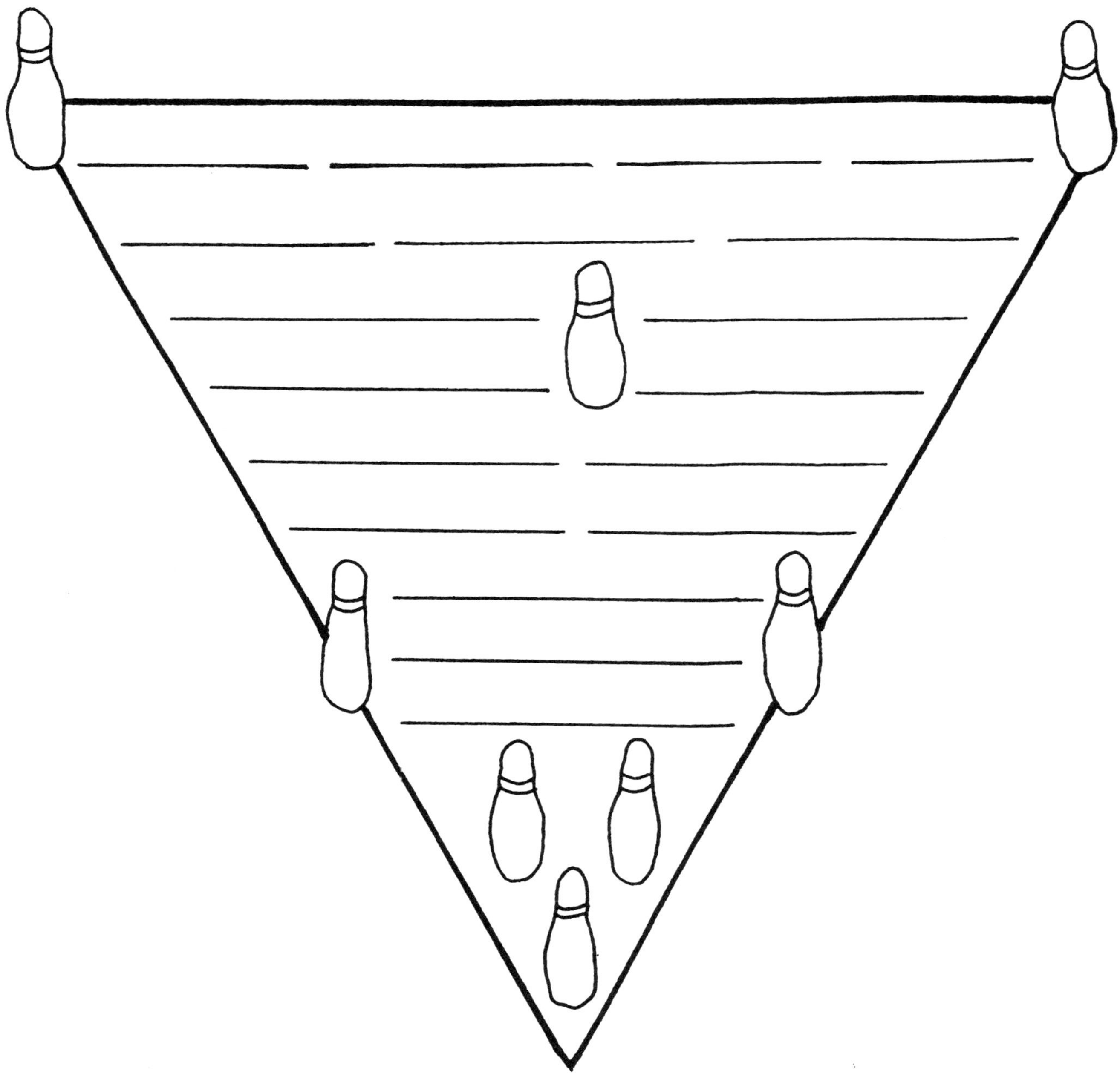

ALTERNATIVE HOMEWORK Do both activities above.

Copy the words your teacher gives you under Classroom Words. Fold this page back along the dotted line so that only the Pretest column shows. Write the words your teacher dictates.

Spell*well* Words	Corrections	Pretest
1. altitude	__________	1. __________
2. barometer	__________	2. __________
3. calculator	__________	3. __________
4. category	__________	4. __________
5. continent	__________	5. __________
6. elevator	__________	6. __________
7. geography	__________	7. __________
8. government	__________	8. __________
9. poetry	__________	9. __________
10. political	__________	10. __________
11. refrigerate	__________	11. __________
12. telescope	__________	12. __________
Outlaw Words		
13. frontier	__________	13. __________
14. glacier	__________	14. __________
Classroom Words		
15. __________	__________	15. __________
16. __________	__________	16. __________
17. __________	__________	17. __________
18. __________	__________	18. __________

Compare your words with the spelling list. Write the words you did not know in the Corrections column. If all, or all but one, of the words are correct, use the following for your spelling words: **appetizer, balcony, magnificent, nonfiction, punctuation, satellite,** and **universe.** Write them in the Corrections column along with your Classroom Words; then do the Alternative Homework this week.

Change the following roots into spelling words by adding to them.

scope ______________________

politic ______________________

poet ______________________

front ______________________

Write the spelling words that are related to the words below.

glacial ______________________

calculate ______________________

continental ______________________

categorical ______________________

altitudinal ______________________

elevate ______________________

refrigerator ______________________

Look at the roots below. Write a spelling word plus one other word that contains each root. You may use a dictionary.

graph ______________________ and ______________________

meter ______________________ and ______________________

govern ______________________ and ______________________

Write your Classroom Words in color anywhere on this page.

<u>ALTERNATIVE HOMEWORK</u> In your reading book find 7 words with several syllables that you want to learn. Write them in the Corrections column on page 61. Then write all of your spelling words and their definitions in your personal dictionary.

Read the definitions below. Find the spelling words that fit the meanings and write the syllables in the spaces.

1. Rhymed verse __ __ + __ __ + __ __
2. Unexplored land __ __ __ __ + __ __ __ __
3. Used to group similar things __ __ __ + __ + __ __ + __ __
4. The height above sea level __ __ + __ __ + __ __ __ __
5. Make food cold __ __ + __ __ __ __ + __ __ + __ __ __
6. The study of the earth __ __ + __ + __ __ __ + __ __ __
7. A device for looking at stars __ __ __ + __ + __ __ __ __ __
8. Having to do with politics __ __ + __ __ __ + __ + __ __ __
9. An ice mass moving slowly over land __ __ __ + __ __ __ __
10. The group that runs a country __ __ __ + __ __ __ + __ __ __ __
11. Instrument to measure the pressure of the atmosphere __ __ + __ __ __ + __ + __ __ __
12. Machine that does math functions __ __ __ + __ __ + __ __ + __ __ __
13. Device to carry people from one floor to another __ __ + __ + __ __ + __ __ __
14. One of seven land areas of the world __ __ __ + __ __ + __ __ __ __

Write your Classroom Words in syllables.

____

____

____

____

<u>ALTERNATIVE HOMEWORK</u> Write your spelling words in syllables as above.

Read the headings below. Write one word in each box that fits the category and that starts with the letter at the beginning of the line. (Look at the example.) Use at least one spelling word in each category. You may use a dictionary.

	Words about Elections and Voting	Words about Literature or Books	Words about Nature and the Earth	Instruments and Tools	Things Studied in School
T					
B					
P					
C					
G					

Write your Classroom Words with their meanings.

____

____

____

____

<u>ALTERNATIVE HOMEWORK</u> Write a story about a visit to a new frontier in Outer Space. Tell about the journey there, what you saw and did while you were there, and how and why you returned to Earth.

In this puzzle you will review words from Lessons 7–13. Write the words in the boxes. Then find the secret message by reading the dark boxes going down the page. The numbers tell which lessons the words come from.

1. We like to play soccer at _____. (8)
2. Which _____ party does that candidate belong to? (13)
3. Be careful not to cut yourself with that sharp _____. (12)
4. The model airplane reached an _____ of 250 feet. (13)
5. The oceans were formed thousands of years ago by a melting _____. (13)

6. My baby sister quickly _____ across the floor to the ball. (10)
7. We'll check the _____ to see if there will be a weather change. (13)
8. I enjoy the _____ of Robert Frost. (13)
9. To reach the thirtieth floor quickly, take the _____. (13)
10. We learned about the island of Sri Lanka in _____ class. (13)
11. We watched the eclipse of the moon through the _____. (13)

12. Settlers went West in covered wagons to settle the _____ . (13)
13. You must water the garden _____ during this dry weather. (12)
14. A surprise ice storm can completely _____ an entire crop of oranges. (9)
15. How much does an elephant _____? (11)
16. The _____ spent three weeks in space. (10)

17. It is best to _____ the mayonnaise after you open it. (13)
18. We met our _____ who will lead us through the wilderness. (7)
19. The United States and Canada are on the ____ of North America. (13)

20. Large herds of _____ still live in northern Scandinavia. (11)
21. My older brother likes to give me _____ about everything. (8)
22. To play this game, choose a _____ : animal, vegetable, or mineral. (13)
23. This itchy rash is caused by _____ ivy. (9)

Write the secret message hidden in the dark boxes. ______________________________

____

What do you think the message means? ______________________________

____

<u>ALTERNATIVE HOMEWORK</u> Do the puzzle above or make one of your own, using your spelling words.

PROGRESS CHART FOR WEEKLY SPELLING TESTS

Write the number of words you spelled correctly in the box under the lesson number.
Put a dot in the box next to that number.
Draw a line to connect the dots after each test.

	LESSON	1	2	3	4	5	6	7	8	9	10	11	12	13
NUMBER OF WORDS CORRECT	Ex. 16													
18														
17														
16	●													
15														
14														
13														
12														
11														
10														
9														
8														
7														
6														
5														
4														
3														
2														
1														
0														